MW01377926

Red Sox Heroes

Remembering the Boston Red Sox Who Helped Make the 1960s Baseball's *Real* Golden Age

Carroll Conklin

Bright Stone
Press
Lewis Center, Ohio

Red Sox Heroes

Remembering the Boston Red Sox Who Helped Make The 1960s Baseball's *Real* Golden Age

Carroll Conklin

Published by

Bright Stone Press

© 2013 Carroll C Conklin

All Rights Reserved.

ISBN-13: 978-1484071373

ISBN-10: 1484071379

No part of this book may be reproduced, stored in or introduced into a retrieval system, or transmitted, in any form or by any means (electronic, mechanical, photocopying, recording or otherwise) without the prior written permission of the copyright owner.

Photo Credits –
Front & Back Covers – **Topps Chewing Gum Inc.**
Topps Chewing Gum Inc. – 6, 8, 9, 10, 12, 14, 15, 16, 17, 19, 20, 21, 24, 27, 28, 29, 30, 32, 33, 36, 37, 38, 39, 41, 42, 43, 44, 45, 46, 47, 48, 49, 52, 53, 54, 56, 58, 62, 63, 64, 65, 66, 67, 69, 70, 72, 73, 74, 76, 77, 78, 79, 80, 81, 83, 85, 87, 88, 90, 92, 94, 95, 96, 97, 98, 100, 104, 105, 108, 110, 111, 113, 114, 115, 118, 119
Baseball Digest – 26, 59, 71, 86

The photos used in this book are in the public domain because their sources were published in the United States between 1923 and 1963 with a copyright notice and the copyrights were not renewed. A search of the The United States Copyright Office Online Catalog for records from 1978 to the present revealed no renewals for the above cited photo sources within the required period for filing.

Contents

Foreword

Why We Still Care About the Baseball Heroes of the 1960s.

These were the heroes who owned the summers of the 1960s.

They were special players at a special time ... when the rules were the same for both leagues, and the only thing that truly separated the American League from the National League was pride.

They played in a decade when greatness flourished ... when some of the game's best hurlers dominated in their prime, and when emerging future pitching stars were just beginning to show the promise that would lead, for some, to Cooperstown. When some of the game's best-ever power hitters smashed fences and records despite having to bat against the best collective pitching baseball had seen since the end of the deadball era.

These were the summers of the 1960s, when the heroes of Boston wore Red Sox uniforms. On their best days (which were, admittedly, too few except for 1967), they were both entertaining and inspiring. They smote hated rivals and sent their best talent to the All-Star game, when those games really were classics, fueled by pride and by knowing that the chance to prove one league's superiority came only twice a year ... in a mid-summer "exhibition" and in the World Series.

On their worst days, they broke our hearts, squandering late-inning leads and pre-season hopes.

They were the heroes of our youth. Yastrzemski and Lonborg. Malzone and Radatz. Petrocelli and Monbouquette. Conigliaro and Harrelson.

And of course, there were heroes that only Red Sox fans could truly appreciate and cherish. Players like Don Schwall and Carroll Hardy and Pete Runnels.

Players lost in the past, but never really forgotten.

Enjoy the memories.

April 8, 2013

Red Sox Managers of the 1960s

Pinky Higgins	1955–1962
Johnny Pesky	1963–1964
Billy Herman	1964–1966
Dick Williams	1967–1969

Johnny Pesky

Billy Herman

Dick Williams

The Infielders

Jerry Adair

Jerry Adair played in the major leagues for 13 seasons. He was known for excellent defense and his toughness, especially as an out in clutch situations and as a player who was lineup-ready day in and day out.

Adair was signed by the Baltimore Orioles in 1958 off the campus of Oklahoma State University. He appeared in 11 games with the Orioles at the end of that season, batting .105, and appeared in 12 games at the end of the 1959 season, batting .314.

Adair made the Orioles' roster for keeps in 1961, batting .264 with 9 home runs and 37 RBIs. He was the Orioles' everyday second

baseman for 6 seasons. Adair's best year came in 1965, when he batted .259 with 7 home runs and 66 RBIs. He led American League second basemen in fielding percentage in both 1964 and 1965, and set records in 1965 for consecutive errorless games by a second baseman (89) and consecutive chances handled without an error (458).

In June of 1966, Adair was traded to the Chicago White Sox for Eddie Fisher. He batted .243 for Chicago over the rest of that season, and a June later was traded to the Boston Red Sox for reliever Don McMahon. He was an important pickup for the Red Sox in their 1967 pennant push, batting .291 with 13 doubles and 26 RBIs in 89 games with Boston.

Adair hit .216 for the Red Sox in 1968, and then was selected by the Kansas City Royals in the expansion draft. He batted .250 for Kansas City in 1969, and drove in 48 runs, the second highest total of his career. He played in 7 games for the Royals in 1970 before being released. He retired as a player after a season in Japan.

Adair batted .254 for his career with 1,022 hits. His only post-season appearance came in 1967, when he batted .125 for Boston in the 1968 World Series.

Jerry Adair

Acquired midway through the 1967 season, Adair was an important part of the Boston pennant drive, batting .291 for the Red Sox.

Eddie Bressoud

Eddie Bressoud was a shortstop with 4 teams through a 12-year major league career. Bressoud was signed by the New York Giants in 1950 and made his major league debut in 1956. He was primarily a backup shortstop for the Giants, hitting .225 with 9 home runs and 43 runs

batted in during the 1960 season. In 1961 he was the initial pick of the Houston Colt .45s in the expansion draft and then was traded to the Boston Red Sox, where he was installed as the everyday shortstop.

Bressoud batted .277 in 1962 with 14 home runs and 68 RBIs. In 1963 he hit 20 home runs with 60 runs batted in. He batted a career-best .293 with 41 doubles, 15 home runs and 55 RBIs in 1964. In 1965 he was traded to the New York Mets for Joe Christopher, and in 1967 was part of a 6-player deal with the St. Louis Cardinals.

In 12 major league seasons, he batted .252 with 925 hits, including 184 doubles and 94 home runs.

Joe Foy

Joe Foy was signed by the Minnesota Twins in 1962, but was selected in that year's minor league draft by the Boston Red Sox. He was the Most Valuable Player of the International League in 1965, hitting .302 to win that league's batting title.

Foy made his major league debut in 1966. He had an excellent rookie season that year, batting .262 with 15 home runs and 63 RBIs while scoring 97 runs. The third baseman hit 16 home runs with 49 RBIs in 1967 and hit 10 home runs with 60 RBIs in 1968.

Selected by the Kansas City Royals in the 1968 expansion draft, Foy batted .262 for the Royals in 1969, with 11 home runs and 71 RBIs. After a single season in Kansas City, he was traded to the New York Mets for Bob Johnson and Amos Otis. Foy batted .236 for the Mets in 1970, with 6 home runs and 37 RBIs. He played 41 games for the Washington Senators in 1971, batting .234. It was his last stop in the major leagues. Foy batted .248 in a 6-year major league career.

Pumpsie Green

Pumpsie Green was the first black player to play for the Red Sox, the last pre-expansion major league team to integrate. Green made his debut with the Red Sox in 1959, playing mostly as a pinch runner and

utility infielder. He appeared in 133 games in 1962, batting .242 with 2 home runs and 21 RBIs. In 1961 he batted .260 with 6 home runs and 27 RBIs for the Red Sox.

In 1962 he was traded with pitcher Tracy Stallard to the New York Mets for Felix Mantilla. He appeared in 17 games for the Mets in 1963, batting .278. It was his last season in the major leagues. Green finished his 5-season career with a .246 batting average.

Tony Horton

Tony Horton was signed by the Boston Red Sox in 1962 and made his major league debut with Boston as a 19-year-old first baseman in 1964, hitting .222 in 36 games. In 1967 he was traded with Don Demeter to the Cleveland Indians for pitcher Gary Bell. He was installed at first base by the Tribe and responded by batting .281 with 10 home runs and 44 RBIs.

Horton batted .249 with 14 home runs and 59 RBIs in 1968, and then had a breakout season in 1969, batting .278 with 27 home runs and 93 RBIs. He batted .269 with 17 home runs and 59 RBIs in 1970 before retiring. In 7 major league seasons, Horton batted .268 with 597 hits and 76 home runs.

Eddie Kasko

Eddie Kasko was the typical 1960s shortstop – good fielding, marginal if any hitting – only he was better than most in the field.

Kasko was signed in 1948 by the St. Louis Browns. It took 9 years of minor league seasoning to ready Kasko (and, especially, his bat) for the big leagues, and he hit .273 for the Cardinals during his rookie season. Two years later he was traded with Del Ennis and Bob Mabe to the Cincinnati Reds for George Crowe, Alex Grammas and Alex Kellner.

It was in Cincinnati that Kasko enjoyed the most success as an everyday player, both with his bat and in the field. He teamed with second baseman Don Blasingame to give Reds pitchers a formidable doubleplay pair behind them. He hit .292 for the Reds in 1960, and batted .271 during Cincinnati's pennant year of 1961. Kasko's best year as a hitter was 1962, when he batted .278 but hit 26 doubles with 41 RBIs.

By 1963, however, Kasko was forced to move over to third base to make way for Leo Cardenas, a shortstop who could match Kasko's range and beat him in the batter's box. A great shortstop with a light stick can be tolerated. A third baseman hitting .241 cannot.

In 1963, the Reds dealt Kasko to the Houston Colt .45's for Jim Dickson, Wally Wolf and cash. After 2 seasons in Houston, Kasko was traded to the Boston Red Sox for infielder Felix Mantilla. He was a utility infielder for the Red Sox in 1966, and retired after hitting .213 that season.

In his 10 years in the major leagues, Kasko hit .213. He was a National League All-Star in 1961.

Frank Malzone

For a decade from the mid 1950s to the mid 1960s, Frank Malzone gave the Boston Red Sox solid play at third base while providing average and power in the middle of the Red Sox batting order. He was a Boston institution whose hitting contributions were generally under-valued as he played in the shadows of a pair of future Hall of Famers, Ted Williams and Carl Yastrzemski.

Born in the Bronx, Malzone was signed by the Red Sox in 1947. After serving an apprenticeship in minor league and 2 years of military service, he played his first full season with Boston in 1957, with a .292 batting average, 31 doubles, 15 home runs and 103 runs batted in. He was runner-up to New York Yankees shortstop Tony Kubek for Rookie of the Year honors in 1957. He followed up in 1958 by batting .295 with 15 home runs and 87 RBIs, and hit .280 in 1959 with 19 homers and 92 RBIs. His 34 doubles were second in the American League (to shortstop Harvey Kuenn of the Detroit Tigers).

From 1960 through 1963, Malzone was the model of consistency for the Red Sox, batting .278 and averaging 16 home runs and 83 RBIs per season. His best season in the 1960s came in 1962, when he batted .283 with 21 home runs and 95 RBIs.

There was a sharp decline in Malzone's power numbers after the 1963 season. In 1965, he was released by the Red Sox and signed with the California Angels. He appeared in 82 games with the Angels in

15

1966, hitting .206 with 2 home runs and 12 RBIs. He retired following the 1966 season.

In 12 seasons, Malzone batted .274 with 1,486 hits, including 239 doubles and 133 home runs. He was named to the American League All-Star team 6 times, and was a 3-time Gold Glove winner.

Frank Malzone
Averaged 90 RBIs per season for the Red Sox from 1957 through 1962.

Felix Mantilla

Infielder Felix Mantilla came up through the Negro and minor leagues with an outfielder named Hank Aaron. Both were All-Stars who broke into the major leagues with the Milwaukee Braves. Both built their reputations on home runs. Aaron hit more.

Mantilla was signed by the Braves in 1952 and was a member of the pennant-winning Braves of 1957 and 1958. After 6 seasons as a utility infielder with the Braves, Mantilla was selected by the New York Mets in the 1961 expansion draft. He spent the 1962 season as

the Mets' everyday third baseman, batting .275 with 11 home runs and 59 runs batted in. Following that season, he was traded to the Boston Red Sox for Pumpsie Green and Tracy Stallard.

In Boston, Mantilla's potential and power were unleashed. He batted .315 in 1963 as the team's utility infielder, and then became a starter at second base in 1965, batting .289 with 30 home runs and 64 RBIs. He followed in 1965, his All-Star season, with 18 home runs and 92 RBIs while batting .275.

In the off season, he was traded to the Houston Colt .45s for shortstop Eddie Kasko. With the Colts in 1966, he batted .219 as a part-time player, and then retired at age 31. Mantilla played 11 seasons in the major leagues. He hit .261 in his career on 707 hits, with 89 home runs and 330 RBIs.

Rico Petrocelli

While lighter-hitting shortstops were the trend in the 1960s (once Ernie Banks moved from shortstop to first), the Boston Red Sox had a shortstop who bucked that trend with power and RBIs. Rico Petrocelli was the most lethal offensive threat among American League shortstops in the late 1960s.

Petrocelli was signed by Boston in 1961 and played his entire major league career with the Red Sox. As a rookie in 1965, Petrocelli hit .232 with 13 home runs and 33 RBIs, numbers that would have been considered adequate for a shortstop of Petrocelli's defensive abilities. He increased his home run production to 18 in 1966 and, in Boston's pennant-winning season of 1967, Petrocelli hit .259 with 17 home runs and 66 RBIs. He was selected for the American League All-Star team in 1967, and finished seventeenth in the Most Valuable Player voting at the end of that season.

Petrocelli's best season came 2 years later when he set an American League record for home runs by a shortstop with 40. He also drove in 97 runs and had career highs in hits (159) and batting average (.297). He followed that campaign with 2 more strong seasons, hitting 29 home runs (with 103 RBIs) in 1970 and 28 homers (with 89 RBIs) in 1971. Petrocelli moved to third base in 1971 to accommodate the arrival of Luis Aparicio in Boston. He remained the Red Sox starting third baseman for the next 6 seasons, averaging 14 home runs and 61 RBIs per season.

Petrocelli was known for his offense, which over-shadowed his considerable defensive skills. He led all American League shortstops in fielding percentage in 1968 and 1969, and led all American League third basemen in fielding percentage in 1971.

Petrocelli retired after the 1976 season, his thirteenth in a Boston uniform. A 2-time All-Star, he finished with 210 career home runs, 127 as a shortstop (sixteenth best all-time). His 40 home run season as an American League shortstop has been surpassed only by Alex Rodriguez.

Pete Runnels

Pete Runnels was the 1960s' first two-time batting champion, and the first player ever to win two batting titles while playing two different positions. Runnels broke into the big leagues as a shortstop for the Washington Senators in 1951. Over the next 7 years, splitting his time between shortstop and second base, Runnels hit .274 for Washington, with a high mark of .310 in 1956. He was traded to the Red Sox before the 1958 season, when he hit .322, the second highest average in the league. He also registered a career high 183 hits in his first year with Boston, which was fourth best in the league.

As Boston's starting second baseman, Runnels won his first batting championship in 1960 with a .320 average. Runnels moved

over to first base in 1961, hitting .317 that year. As the Red Sox first baseman in 1962, Runnels claimed his second batting title with a .326 average. In his 5 years with Boston, Pete Runnels was one of the league's most consistent hitters, with a batting average of .320 over that period.

His batting title in 1962 wasn't enough to keep Runnels in a Red Sox uniform, as he was traded in the off season to the Houston Colt .45s for outfielder Roman Mejias. Runnels hit .253 in 1963, his only full season with Houston. He was released 22 games into the 1964 season, and never played again in the majors.

Chuck Schilling

Chuck Schilling was signed by the Boston Red Sox in 1958 and made his major league debut on Opening Day of 1961 as the team's everyday second baseman. Schilling had a strong rookie season for Boston, batting .259 with 5 home runs and 52 RBIs. His defensive capabilities encouraged the Red Sox to move batting champion Pete Runnels to first base to make room for Schilling's glove and range.

An injury to his wrist shortened Schilling's 1962 season and hampered his hitting for the rest of his career. During his 5-season major league career, Schilling batted .239 in 541 games played, with 23 home runs and 146 runs batted in.

Dick Schofield

Dick Schofield was signed by the St. Louis Cardinals in 1953 and made his major league debut later that season. He played in the major

leagues for 19 years with 7 different teams, primarily as a utility infielder, and a very good one.

He was the everyday shortstop for the Pittsburgh Pirates in 1963, batting .246 with 18 doubles and 32 RBIs. He finished his career with a .227 batting average and 699 hits.

George Scott

George Scott was the best defensive first baseman from the mid-1960s to the mid-1970s, winning 8 Gold Gloves within that decade. He was also a slugger who, at one point in his career, was the most productive--and at another point, the least productive--first baseman batting in the American League.

Scott was signed by the Boston Red Sox in 1962 and spent the next 4 years progressing through the Boston farm system. In 1965, he won the Eastern League Triple Crown, leading the league with 25 home runs, 94 RBIs and a .319 batting average. That performance earned Scott a shot at the Red Sox roster, and he stayed in the major leagues for the next 14 years.

Scott hit .245 as a rookie in 1966 with 27 home runs and 90 RBIs. He followed up in 1967 with a .303 batting average, hitting 19 home runs and driving in 82 run. He had a disastrous 1968, batting only .171 with 3 home runs and 25 RBIs, but rebounded in 1969 by hitting .253 with 16 home runs and 52 RBIs.

Scott's most productive period as a hitter came in the 1970s. He hit .296 for the Red Sox in 1970, and slugged 24 home runs with 78 RBIs in 1971.

Following the 1971 season, he was traded with Ken Brett, Billy Conigliaro, Joe Lahoud, Jim Lonborg and Don Pavletich to the Milwaukee Brewers for Pat Skrable, Tommy Harper, Lew Krause and Marty Pattin. In 5 seasons with the Brewers, Scott hit a combined .283 and averaged 23 home runs and 93 RBIs per season. His best season came in 1975, when he hit .285 and led the American League with 109 RBIs. His 36 home runs also tied for the league lead with Reggie Jackson.

Before the 1977 season, Scott was traded back to the Red Sox (with Bernie Carbo) for Cecil Cooper. He hit .269 for Boston that season, with 33 home runs and 95 RBIs. He hit .233 for the Red Sox in 1978, and split the 1979 season with the Red Sox, the Kansas City

Royals and the New York Yankees, hitting a combined .254 with 6 home runs and 49 RBIs. He retired after the 1979 season.

In 14 big league seasons, Scott batted .268 with 271 home runs. He was named to the American League All-Star team 3 times.

Norm Siebern

Tall, athletic and bespectacled, Norm Siebern was a solid hitter who grew up professionally in the New York Yankees organization and blossomed into an All-Star outfielder and first baseman with the Kansas City Athletics. The New York papers--and even Yankees manager Casey Stengel -- occasionally made sport of his quiet demeanor, but there was no question about the quality of his production, at bat and in the field.

Siebern was signed by the Yankees in 1951, and after 2 years in the minors and a military tour, Siebern made his debut with the Yankees in 1956, hitting .204 in 54 games. The well-stocked Yankees outfield left no room for Siebern, so he returned to the minors in

1957, hitting .349 for Denver in the American Association, with 45 doubles, 15 triples, 24 home runs and 118 RBIs. He was named *Sporting News* Minor League Player of the Year for 1957. That performance earned Siebern a permanent place on the Yankees roster in 1958, and he responded with a .300 batting average, 14 home runs and 55 RBIs. Siebern won the Gold Glove for his left field play, but ironically, it was pair of errors in the 1958 World Series that sent him to the bench for most of that Series.

Siebern hit .271 in 1959, and after the season was traded with Hank Bauer, Don Larsen and Marv Throneberry to the Kansas City Athletics for Joe DeMaestri, Kent Hadley and Roger Maris. He hit .279 for the A's in 1960 with 19 home runs and 69 RBIs. His performance was overshadowed by the MVP season that Maris had for the Yankees.

Siebern's hitting kept improving, especially as he spent more time at first base for the A's. He batted .296 in 1961 with 36 doubles, 18 home runs and 98 RBIs. In 1962, Siebern hit .308 (fifth highest in the American League) with 25 doubles, 25 home runs and 117 RBIs (second in the AL to Harmon Killebrew's 126).

Siebern's production fell off slightly in 1963, batting .272 with 16 home runs and 83 RBIs, and after that season he was traded to the Baltimore Orioles for first baseman Jim Gentile. He hit .245 for the Orioles in 1964 with 12 home runs and 56 RBIs, and he led the majors with 106 walks. In 1965, the O's, to make room for Curt Blefary and Paul Blair, moved Boog Powell from the outfield to first base, limiting Siebern's playing time. After that season he was traded to the California Angels for Dick Simpson, whom the Orioles later packaged in the trade for Frank Robinson.

Siebern hit .247 in 1966, his only season with the Angels. He was traded to the San Francisco Giants for outfielder Len Gabrielson, and in July of 1967 was purchased by the Boston Red Sox. A part-time player for Boston, Siebern was released by the Red Sox in August of 1968 and retired. Siebern finished his 12-season career with a .272 batting average. He had 1,217 hits and 132 home runs. He was an All-Star from 1962 through 1964.

Dick Stuart

Dick Stuart was the epitome of the good-hit, no-field first baseman. For nearly a decade in the big leagues, he was one of the game's most feared run producers, and a major liability in the field. If a player was ever made to be a designated hitter, it was Stuart. But he retired 7 seasons before the American League adopted the DH.

Stuart was signed by the Pittsburgh Pirates in 1951, and toiled in the Pirates' minor league organization until his major league in debut

in 1958. He was a hitting terror in the minors, ripping 115 home runs in 1956 and 1957. In 67 games with the Pirates during his rookie season, Stuart hit .268 with 16 home runs, 48 RBIs and a .543 slugging percentage. Stuart also had one error for every 4 games he played at first base, leading all National League first basemen in total errors despite playing only 64 games at first base.

His best year for the Pirates was 1961, hitting .301 with 35 home runs and 117 RBIs. He finished fifth in the league in slugging that year with a .581 average. When his offensive numbers dipped dramatically in 1962 (.228 with 16 home runs and 64 RBIs), Stuart and pitcher Jack Lamabe were traded to the Boston Red Sox for catcher Jim Pagliaroni and pitcher Don Schwall.

A powerful pull hitter, Stuart's swing was made for the "Green Monster" in Fenway Park. He had a career season for Boston in 1963, launching 42 home runs and leading the American League in both

RBIs (118) and total bases (319). He became the first player in major league history to hit 30 or more home runs in each league. He also set the major league record in 1963 with 29 errors at first base (a record that still stands today).

Stuart's numbers the next year were almost as good, as he hit 33 home runs and finished second in the league in RBIs with 114 (Brooks Robinson led with 118). At his peak from 1961 to 1964, Stuart averaged 31 home runs and 103 RBIs per season. He also made every ground ball an adventure at first base, earning him the nickname "Dr. Strangeglove."

After the 1964 season, the Red Sox traded Stuart to the Philadelphia Phillies for pitcher Dennis Bennett. Stuart spent one season with the Phillies, hitting 28 home runs and driving in 95 runs. He split the next season between the New York Mets and Los Angeles Dodgers, and then spent 2 years playing in Japan, closing out his career with the California Angels in 1969.

Dick Stuart

In 1963, Stuart hit 42 home runs for the
Red Sox and led the American League
with 118 RBIs. He also set a record with
29 errors at first base.

Vic Wertz

Vic Wertz played for 17 years in the American League with 5 different teams. After serving in World War II, he broke in as an outfielder with the Detroit Tigers in 1947 and by 1949 was one of the most dangerous power hitters in the league, batting .304 with 20 home runs and 133 RBIs.

He batted .308 with 27 home runs and 123 RBIs in 1950. During the 1950s, playing for the Tigers, the St. Louis Browns and Baltimore Orioles, the Cleveland Indians, and the Boston Red Sox, Wertz hit .277 and averaged 20 home runs and 74 runs batted in per season. His best post-Tiger season came in 1956 with the Indians, when he batted .264 with 32 home runs and 106 RBIs.

In 1958 the Indians traded Wertz with Gary Geiger to the Boston Red Sox for Jim Piersall. He batted .275 for Boston in 1959, and then hit .282 with 19 home runs and 103 RBIs for the Red Sox in 1960. In 1961 he was traded back to the Detroit Tigers, and he split the 1963 season between the Tigers and the Minnesota Twins.

For his career, Wertz hit 266 home runs with 1,178 RBIs, a .469 career slugging average and a .364 career on-base percentage. He had a .277 career batting average and was named to the American League All-Star team 4 times.

Red Sox All-Stars of the 1960s

First Base:

Pete Runnels, 1962

George Scott, 1966

Second Base:

Pete Runnels, 1960

Felix Mantilla, 1965

Third Base:

Frank Malzone, 1960, 1963-1964

Shortstop:

Eddie Bressoud, 1964

Rico Petrocelli, 1967, 1969

Pete Runnels
2-Time All-Star at 2 Positions

Frank Malzone
3-Time All-Star at Third Base

Outfield:

Ted Williams, 1960

Carl Yastrzemski, 1963, 1965-1969

Tony Conigliaro, 1967

Ken Harrelson, 1968

Reggie Smith, 1969

Carl Yastrzemski
6-Time All-Star During the
1960s

Pitcher:

Bill Monbouquette, 1960, 1962-1963

Mike Fornieles, 1961

Don Schwall, 1961

Dick Radatz, 1963-1964

Jim Lonborg, 1967

Jose Santiago, 1968

Gary Bell, 1968

Ray Culp, 1969

Bill Monbouquette
3-Time All-Star

The Outfielders

Joe Christopher

Joe Christopher was signed by the Pittsburgh Pirates in 1955 and made his major league debut 4 years later. The outfielder played parts of 3 seasons with the Pirates, batting a combined .244 before being

selected by the New York Mets in the 1961 expansion draft. He batted .244 for the Mets in 1962, his first full season in the major leagues, with 6 home runs and 32 runs batted in.

His best season came in 1964, when Christopher batted .300 with 16 home runs and 76 RBIs. He batted .249 in 1965 and then was traded to the Boston Red Sox for Eddie Bressoud. He appeared in only 12 games with Boston before being traded with Earl Wilson to the Detroit Tigers for Don Demeter. He never played for the Tigers, and retired at age 30 after 8 major league seasons. Christopher finished with a .260 career batting average.

Lou Clinton

Outfielder Lou Clinton was an important bat in the Boston Red Sox lineup in the early 1960s. He was signed by the Red Sox in 1955 and made his major league debut in 1960, batting .228 as a rookie. He spent most of the 1961 season with Seattle in the Pacific Coast league, hitting .295 with 21 home runs and 102 RBIs.

That performance earned Clinton a full-time shot with the 1962 Red Sox, and he delivered. Clinton batted .294 in 1962 with 18 home runs and 75 RBIs. His 10 triples were second-highest in the American League. (Gino Cimoli led the league with 15 triples.)

In 1963, Clinton's 22 home runs and 77 runs batted in were second highest on the team (to Dick Stuart in both categories). His batting average, however, slipped to .232. Clinton batted .251 in 1964 (with 12 home runs and 44 RBIs), and during the season was traded to the Los Angeles Angels for first baseman Lee Thomas. He batted .243 for the Angels in 1965, and also played with the Kansas City A's and Cleveland Indians that season. Prior to the 1966 season, he was traded to the New York Yankees for catcher Doc Edwards. He hit .220 for the Yankees in 1966, and retired in 1967 at age 29.

Clinton played for 5 different teams in his 7-year major league career. He finished with 532 hits and a .247 career batting average.

Tony Conigliaro

With acknowledgement of the fatal pitch that felled Cleveland Indians shortstop Ray Chapman in 1920, the next most devastating bean ball in major league history was delivered on August 18, 1967. The victim of that fastball was Tony Conigliaro, a phenomenal young slugger whose career was tragically derailed that August evening.

Conigliaro was signed in 1962 by the Boston Red Sox at age 17. Two years later, he was the starting right fielder for the Bosox. He hit .290 with 54 RBIs that season. He also set major league records for a teenager with 24 home runs and a .530 slugging average.

The next year, Conigliaro was even better. His 32 home runs were tops in the American League in 1965, making Conigliaro the youngest player (at age 20) ever to win the home run crown. He followed in 1966 with 28 home runs and 93 RBIs, establishing him one of the league's most feared sluggers by age 21.

In 1967, Conigliaro picked up where he left off the previous year. By mid-August, only 95 games into the season, he already had 20 home runs and 67 RBIs (with a .287 batting average and .519 slugging percentage) when he struck in the face by a pitched ball. He was carried off the field on a stretcher, sustaining a broken cheekbone and severe damage to his left retina. Largely as a result of his injuries, the major leagues adopted the style of batting helmet with the protective ear flap that is standard today.

Because of persisting problems with his vision, Conigliaro didn't play again until 1969. He hit 20 home runs with 82 RBIs during his "Comeback Player of the Year" season in 1969, and actually recorded his career-best power numbers in 1970 with 36 home runs and 116 RBIs. But permanent deterioration of his eyesight limited his playing ability thereafter. He was traded to the California Angels prior to the 1971 season, when he hit only 4 home runs in 74 games. He attempted another comeback with the Red Sox in 1975, but his career was over by age 30.

In 1990, the Boston Red Sox instituted The Tony Conigliaro Award to honor the memory of Tony Conigliaro (he passed away that year after suffering a heart attack and stroke in 1982). The award is given annually to the player who best overcomes an obstacle and adversity through the attributes of spirit, determination and courage.

Don Demeter

Don Demeter's well-traveled major league career had plenty of ups and downs. His best "ups" ranked him among the most productive hitters in baseball.

Demeter was signed by the Brooklyn Dodgers in 1953 and finally broke into the Dodgers lineup as a regular in 1959, hitting 18 home runs with 70 RBIs for that season's World Series champions. At the start of the 1961 season, the Dodgers traded Demeter with Charley Smith to the Philadelphia Phillies for pitcher Dick Farrell and infielder Joe Koppe. In Philadelphia, Demeter came into his prime, hitting 21 home runs with 70 RBIs for the 1961 season. In 1962, he batted .307 with 29 home runs and 107 RBIs. His power numbers slipped slightly in 1963, as Demeter finished the year with 22 home runs and 83 RBIs.

In December of 1963, the Phillies traded Demeter and pitcher Jack Hamilton to the Detroit Tigers for pitcher Jim Bunning and catcher Gus Triandos. It may be the best trade the Phillies ever made. Bunning, who had already won 100 games in the American League, went on to become the first 100-game winner in both leagues en route to a Hall of Fame career. Demeter, the centerpiece of the trade for Detroit, went on to hit 22 home runs for the Tigers with 80 RBIs in 1964. His offensive numbers would never be that robust again. Demeter slipped to 16 home runs and 58 RBIs in 1965, and in 1966 he was involved in a trade for another starting pitcher, moving to the Boston Red Sox for Earl Wilson. Wilson blossomed into a 20-game winner for the Tigers, while Demeter's offensive stats continued to decline. Demeter spent a little over one season with the Red Sox, and closed out his career with the Cleveland Indians in 1967.

Gary Geiger

Gary Geiger was a speedy outfielder who managed to string together a 12-season major league career despite several injuries and physical ailments that limited his performance on the field. Nevertheless, he was a talented athlete with speed on the base paths, and a fan favorite wherever he played.

Geiger was signed as a pitcher and as an outfielder by the St. Louis Cardinals in 1954. In 1957, he was drafted by the Cleveland Indians (as an outfielder) and made his major league debut in a Tribe uniform in 1958, batting .231 in 91 games his rookie season. There was little room for Geiger in a Cleveland outfield that already featured Rocky Colavito, Roger Maris, Carroll Hardy and the recently acquired Minnie Minoso, so the Indians dealt Geiger and Vic Wertz to the Boston Red Sox for Jim Piersall. Geiger hit .245 for the Red Sox in 1959 and .302 in 1960. However, both of those seasons were abbreviated by health problems. He appeared in only 77 games in 1960 due to a collapsed lung.

Geiger managed to play a full season in 1961, batting .232 and leading the Red Sox with 18 home runs. He batted .249 in 1962 and then hit .263 in 1963, but those would be his last seasons as a full-time player. On- and off-the-field health problems limited his playing time for the rest of his career. He played for 2 seasons with the Atlanta Braves and one season with the Houston Astros before retiring after 5 games in the 1970 season. Geiger finished his career with a .246 lifetime batting average.

Lenny Green

Lenny Green was good enough to forge a 12-year major league career based on speed and solid center field play. But he was not quite good enough to keep from being replaced and traded repeatedly, and often traded by a team just before it celebrated post-season success.

Green was signed by the Baltimore Orioles and made brief appearances with the team in 1957 and 1958. Two months into the 1959 season, he was traded by the Baltimore Orioles to the Washington Senators for Albie Pearson. He hit .242 for the Senators as a spare outfielder in 1959, and followed up in 1960 by batting .294 with a career-best 21 stolen bases. When the team moved to the Twin Cities, Green had his best seasons with a bat. He hit .285 in 1961 with 28 doubles, 9 home runs and 50 RBIs. He followed up in 1962 by  batting .271 with 33 doubles (eighth best in the American League), 14 home runs and 63 RBIs.

In 1963, Green lost his starting job in centerfield to Jimmie Hall. He hit .239 as a part-time player, and was traded in 1964 to the Los Angeles Angels (with first baseman Vic Power) in a deal that sent Jerry Kindall to the Twins. Before the end of the 1964 season, he was purchased by the Orioles. He hit a combined .211 for the 1964 season.

The Boston Red Sox purchased Green in 1965, and he batted .276 as Boston's starting center fielder that season. He spent one more season in Boston (batting .241 in only 85 games), before being purchased by the Detroit Tigers. He was a pinch hitter and utility outfielder for the Tigers in 1967, batting .278. Green retired after being released 6 games into the 1968 season. He finished his career with 788 hits and a .267 lifetime batting average.

He played for Minnesota, Boston and Detroit one season before each of those teams won the American League pennant. Green's career was built on speed, but repeatedly fell short in timing.

Carroll Hardy

Outfielder Carroll Hardy has the distinction of being the only player to pinch-hit for both Carl Yastrzemski and Ted Williams. On September 20, 1960, Williams' final season, the Hall of Famer fouled a batted ball off his foot, and left the game. Hardy finished the at-bat, making him officially Williams' pinch hitter. Hardy lined into a double play.

Batting for Yastrzemski in May of 1961, Hardy bunted for a single in the eighth inning of a 7-6 loss to the New York Yankees. He moved to second on a walk to Jackie Jensen and scored on Frank Malzone's single to center field. Hardy played left field in the ninth inning and batted again in the bottom of the ninth. He reached first on an error by Yankee shortstop Tony Kubek.

Hardy played 8 seasons in the major leagues with Boston, Cleveland, Houston and Minnesota. He had a career batting average of .225, with a career best .263 in 1961.

One final note about Carroll Hardy's career as a pinch hitter: as a member of the Cleveland Indians, Hardy also pinch hit for Roger Maris in 1958, hitting a home run off Billy Pierce.

Ken Harrelson

"Free spirit" would be an understatement when describing the unpredictable Ken Harrelson. An All-Star talent combined with steel-like independence, Harrelson put up outstanding power hitting numbers at his best, and walked away from his playing career while still near its peak ... apparently because he felt like it.

Harrelson was signed by the Kansas City Athletics in 1959 and made his debut in an A's uniform 4 years later. His first full major league season came in 1965, when he led the Athletics with 23 home runs and 66 RBIs. He was traded to the Washington Senators in June of 1966, and was purchased back by the A's a year later.

His second tour in Kansas City lasted only 2 months. When A's owner Charles Finley fired manager Alvin Dark, Harrelson went public to protest Dark's dismissal, calling Finley "a menace to baseball." Finley released Harrelson outright, which turned out to be a career break for the outfielder.

As a free agent, Harrelson signed a lucrative contract with the Boston Red Sox. He was a key addition to Boston's successful 1967 pennant drive, hitting 3 home runs with 14 RBIs down the stretch for the Red Sox.

In 1968, Harrelson had his best season, hitting 35 home runs and leading the majors with 109 RBIs. He started well in 1969, but after 10 games was surprisingly traded with pitchers Dick Ellsworth and Juan Pizarro to the Cleveland Indians for Joe Azcue, Vicente Romo and Sonny Siebert. He finished the season hitting 30 home runs with 92 RBIs playing for the team with the worst record in the American League.

During the following spring training, Harrelson suffered a broken leg while sliding into second base. He sat out most of the 1970 season with the injury, returning only for the final 17 games and hitting only one home run. When he returned for the 1971 campaign, Harrelson found Chris Chambliss firmly entrenched as the Indians' first baseman. He played in 52 games for the Tribe that season, hitting 5 home runs and driving in 14 runs, and then abruptly retired to pursue a career as a professional golfer.

In 9 major league seasons, Harrelson hit 131 home runs while batting .239. After retiring as a player (and as a professional golfer), Harrelson had a long career as a baseball broadcaster, with a stint as general manager of the Chicago White Sox.

Jackie Jensen

A 3-time American League RBI champion, Jackie Jensen played only one season in the 1960s. The 3-time All-Star had been the league's Most Valuable Player in 1958, batting .286 with 35 home runs and a league-leading 122 RBIs. He led the league again with 112 RBIs in 1959, and won a Gold Glove, and then retired after 10 major league seasons at age 32 due to his fear of flying.

Jensen sat out the 1960 season and tried to make a comeback in 1961, batting .263 with 13 home runs and 66 RBIs. Then he promptly retired for the second and last time. Jensen started his career with the New York Yankees and was traded to the Washington Senators in 1952. He was traded to Boston in 1953, and batted .282 in 7 seasons with the Red Sox. Over his 11-year career, Jensen compiled a career batting average of .279 with 199 home runs and 929 runs batted in.

Jim Landis

During his 11-year major league career, Jim Landis was an outstanding center fielder who could also hit for average and occasional power. He was signed by the Chicago White Sox in 1952 and spent the next 5 years working his way through the White Sox farm system (after 2 years of military service). He debuted with the White Sox in 1957 at the age of 23, batting .212 in 96 games.

He became the regular center fielder for the White Sox in 1958, batting .277 with 15 home runs and 64 RBIs. From 1958 through 1963, Landis batted a combined .258 while averaging 13 home runs and 61 RBIs per season. His most productive season offensively came in 1961, when he batted .283 with 22 home runs and 85 RBIs. He also won his second of 5 consecutive Gold Gloves that season.

After 8 years in Chicago, Landis was sent to the Kansas City Athletics (with Mike Hershberger and Fred Talbot) in a 3-team deal that brought Tommie Agee, Tommy John and John Romano to the White Sox while sending Rocky Colavito to the Cleveland Indians. Landis hit .239 for the A's in 1965, and then was traded to the Indians for Phil Roof and Joe Rudi. Landis batted .222 for Cleveland in 1966, and spent 1967 playing for 3 teams. He was traded by the Indians with Doc Edwards and Jim Weaver to the Houston Astros for Lee Maye and Ken Retzer. Then in June he was traded by the Astros to the Detroit Tigers for Larry Sherry. The Tigers released Landis in August and he signed as a free agent with the

Boston Red Sox. He spent a week in Boston, and then was released. He hit a combined .237 for the 1967 season.

Landis retired after 11 major league seasons with a career batting average of .247. He was a member of the American League All-Star team in 1962.

Jim Landis
One of the great American League center fielders of the 1960s, Landis closed out his 11-year career with the Red Sox.

Don Lock

Don Lock was a lanky right-handed batter who hit with substantial power but would never compete for a batting title. He was also an excellent outfielder and a fixture in the Washington Senators' line-up in the early-to-mid 1960s.

Lock was signed by the New York Yankees in 1958 and spent 4 seasons in the Yankees' minor league system before being traded in 1962 to the Senators for first baseman Dale Long. He appeared in 71 games for the Senators in 1962, batting .253 with 12 home runs and 37 RBIs while patrolling left field.

In 1963, Lock was installed as the Senators' starting center fielder and responded by hitting .252 with 27 home runs and 82 RBIs. In 1964, he had a nearly identical season, batting .248 with 28 homers and 80 RBIs.

American league pitchers finally caught up with Lock in 1965, and he hit only 16 home runs in each of the next 2 seasons, averaging 43 RBIs. Following the 1966 season, he was traded to the Philadelphia Phillies for pitcher Darold Knowles and responded by batting .252 in 1967 with 14 home runs and 51 RBIs. He would play 2 more seasons, in Philadelphia and with the Boston Red Sox, hitting a total of 9 home runs with 36 RBIs. He retired after the 1969 season with a .238 career batting average and 122 home runs.

Roman Mejias

A native of Cuba, outfielder Roman Mejias was signed by the Pittsburgh Pirates in 1953. He batted over .300 in his first 2 seasons in the Pirates' farm system, and made his debut in Pittsburgh in 1955, batting .216 in 71 games with 3 home runs and 21 RBIs. He spent the next 6 seasons up and down from Pittsburgh to the minors, batting a combined .253 and showing flashes of power, especially during his minor league tours at Columbus in the International League. But there was no place for Mejias in the Pirates outfield of the early 1960s, and in October of 1961 he became the eleventh pick of the Houston Colt .45s in the expansion draft.

In Houston, Mejias (now age 31) finally had the opportunity to show what kind of full-time player he could be at the major league level. In 1962, he batted .286 with 24 home runs and 76 RBIs, leading the team in all 3 offensive categories.

His career in Houston (and as an everyday player) was short-lived. In November of 1962, he was traded to the Boston Red Sox for first baseman and reigning American League batting champion Pete Runnels. In Boston, Mejias was relegated to a back-up role in the outfield, playing behind Gary Geiger and Lou Clinton (as well as future Hall of Famer Carl Yastrzemski). He batted .227 for the Red Sox as a part-timer in 1963, with only 11 home runs and 39 RBIs. In 1964 he appeared in only 62 games for the Red Sox, batting .238 with 2 home runs and 4 RBIs. It was his last season in the major leagues (though he did play one more year in Japan).

In 9 major league seasons, Mejias batted .254 with 54 home runs and 202 RBIs.

Floyd Robinson

Fleet Floyd Robinson was a fixture in the Chicago White Sox outfield in the early 1960s. A solid hitter and sure-handed outfielder, Robinson was the offensive lynchpin for a White Sox team that, from 1963 to 1965, was the second-best American League team ... to both the New York Yankees and the Minnesota Twins.

Robinson played semi-pro and minor league baseball from 1954 through 1957 when his team at the time, San Diego in the Pacific Coast League, became the AAA affiliate of first the Cleveland Indians and then the Chicago White Sox. The White Sox brought Robinson up for the last month of the 1960 season and he remained a starting outfielder for Chicago for 7 seasons. He hit .310 in his rookie campaign of 1961, finishing third in balloting for the Rookie-of-the-Year award behind Don Schwall and Dick Howser.

Robinson hit .312 in 1962, with 11 home runs, 10 triples and 109 RBIs. He led the American League with 45 doubles. His batting average slipped to .283 in 1963, but he rebounded to hit .301 in 1964.

In both of those seasons, the White Sox finished second to the Yankees. Those White Sox teams were known for excellent pitching that carried a suspect offensive lineup. Robinson's bat was critical to that lineup, and when his hitting productivity started to decline in 1965 (.265 batting average with 14 home runs and 66 RBIs), his days in

Chicago became numbered. He hit .237 in 1966 and was dealt to the Cincinnati Reds for left-handed pitcher Jim O'Toole.

Robinson never regained the hitting magic from earlier in his career. He hit only .238 for the Reds in 1967 and batted .219 combined for the Oakland A's and Boston Red Sox in 1968. He retired following the 1968 season with a career batting average of .283.

Floyd Robinson

A .287 hitter in 7 seasons with the Chicago White Sox, Robinson had little left in his bat when he joined the Red Sox in 1968 for his final big league campaign.

Al Smith

Outfielder Al Smith was traded 3 times during his 12-year major league career. In the first 2 of those trades, to Chicago and to Baltimore, Smith had the distinction of being traded with a future Hall of Famer. He also distinguished himself as a good hitter whose legs and bat produced plenty of runs.

Smith was signed by the Cleveland Indians in 1948 and made his debut in Cleveland in 1953, hitting .240 in 47 games. He opened the 1954 season as the Indians' starting left-fielder, batting .281 for the American League champions. He scored 101 runs and led the team in doubles with 29.

In 1955, Smith led the American League by scoring 123 runs. He batted .306 with 22 home runs and 77 RBIs, and was named to the American League All-Star team. He finished third in the Most Valuable Player balloting for that season.

Smith played 2 more seasons with the Indians and then was traded (with future Hall of Famer Early Wynn) to the Chicago White Sox for Minnie Minoso and Fred Hatfield. He struggled in his first 2 seasons in Chicago, batting .252 in 1958 and .237 in 1959. He bounced back in 1960, hitting .315 with 31 doubles, 12 home runs and 72 RBIs. In 1961, he posted the best power numbers of his career, hitting 28 home runs with 93 RBIs.

Smith's last season in Chicago was 1962, when he batted .292 with 16 home runs and 82 RBIs. In the off-season, he was traded with another future Hall of Famer, shortstop Luis Aparicio, to the

Baltimore Orioles for Ron Hansen, Dave Nicholson, Pete Ward and Hoyt Wilhelm. He batted .272 for the Orioles in 1963, but with only 10 home runs and 39 RBIs. He was involved in one more trade, returning to Cleveland in exchange for Willie Kirkland. He split the 1964 season between the Indians and the Boston Red Sox, batting a combined .176. He retired in 1964 at age 36.

Smith finished with a career batting average of .272 with 1,458 hits. He scored 843 runs with 258 doubles, 164 home runs and 676 RBIs. He was a member of the American League All-Star team twice.

Al Smith

Batted .272 over his 12-year major
league career.

Reggie Smith

Reggie Smith was one of the most under-rated all-around players of the late 1960s and early 1970s. During a 17-year major league career, he hit .300 or better 7 times, and led the American League in doubles twice.

Yet he was never fully recognized as a power hitter and run producer, and was never viewed as the best player on the 4 major league teams he played for. He was simply a valuable hitter and fielder (with a strong throwing arm) who did his job well day in and day out. In 13 seasons he played at least 70 games, and in each of those seasons his team had a winning record.

Smith was signed by the Minnesota Twins in June of 1963 and selected by the Boston Red Sox in the first-year draft in December of that year. He spent the next 3 seasons in the Red Sox farm system, winning the International League batting title in 1966.

Smith played in 158 games as a rookie in the Red Sox pennant-winning season of 1967, hitting for a .246 average with 15 home runs and 61 RBIs. He finished second to Minnesota's Rod Carew in the Rookie of the Year voting.

The switch-hitting Smith batted .265 in 1968, leading the American League with 37 doubles. He hit .309 in 1969 (second in the league to Carew's .322), with 25 home runs and 93 RBIs. In his 7 full seasons with the Red Sox, Smith batted a combined .281. His best offensive season in Boston was 1971, when he hit .283 with 30 home runs and 96 RBIs. He also led the league with 33 doubles.

Following the 1973 season, Smith was traded with Ken Tatum to the St. Louis Cardinals for Bernie Carbo and Rick Wise. In his first season with the Cardinals, Smith hit .309 with 23 home runs and 100 RBIs. He batted .302 in 1975, and during the 1976 season was traded to the Los Angeles Dodgers. Over the next 6 seasons, he batted .297. In 1977, he had a career-high 32 home runs while hitting .307 for the

Dodgers. He followed up in 1978 with a .295 batting average, 29 home runs and 93 RBIs.

Smith appeared in 4 World Series, batting a combined .247. In the 1967 Series against the Cardinals, Smith had 2 home runs and 3 RBIs for the Red Sox. In the 6-game 1977 World Series against the New York Yankees, Smith hit .273 with 3 home runs and 5 RBIs for the Dodgers.

Smith finished his career in 1982 with the San Francisco Giants, batting .284. He collected 2,020 hits and was a 7-time All-Star. He also won a Gold Glove in 1968.

Jose Tartabull

Jose Tartabull's stock in trade was speed, on the base paths and in the outfield. He made runs happen with his feet.

Tartabull was signed by the San Francisco Giants in 1958, and spent 4 seasons in the Giants' farm system until his trade to the Kansas City Athletics in 1961 for catcher Joe Pignatano. He hit .277 as a rookie in 1962, stealing 19 bases, fifth best in the American League.

From 1963 through 1965, Tartabull shuttled between Kansas City and the Athletics' Triple-A affiliates in the Pacific Coast League. He hit .273 in 93 games with Vancouver in 1965 before being called back to Kansas City, where he batted .312 in 68 games for the A's with 11 doubles and 11 stolen bases.

In June of 1966, Tartabull was traded by the A's with Rollie Sheldon and John Wyatt to the Boston Red Sox for Jim Gosger, Guido Grilli and Ken Sanders. He took over center field, hitting .277 for the Red Sox, and followed up in Boston's pennant-winning season of 1967 by batting .223. He hit .281 as a part-time outfielder for Boston in 1968, and then was sold back to the Athletics.

Tartabull hit .290 for the A's in 1969, and retired after 24 games during the 1970 season. In 9 big league seasons, Tartabull posted a career batting average of .261.

Lee Thomas

When Lee Thomas was signed by the New York Yankees in 1954, he looked like someone destined for pinstripe greatness. A left-handed batter who could hit for average and power, Thomas put up impressive minor league numbers as he progressed through the Yankees' farm system, hitting 25 home runs with 122 RBIs in 1959 and 28 home runs with 112 RBIs in 1960.

The only thing standing in Thomas' way was the powerful Yankees lineup of the late 1950s. A month into the 1961 season, Thomas was traded by the Yankees with Ryne Duren and Johnny James to the Los Angeles Angels for Bob Cerv and Tex Clevenger. It was in Los Angeles that he became a hitting star, almost overnight. Despite appearing in only 130 games, Thomas was third on the team in home runs (24 to Leon Wagner's 28) and RBIs (70 to Ken Hunt's 84) and second on the team with a .284 batting average (trailing only Albie Pearson's .288).

In 1962, when the fledgling Angels shocked the American League by finishing third, Thomas led the team in batting average at .290. He hit 26 home runs with 104 RBIs. His offensive production slipped significantly in 1963, and during the 1964 campaign Thomas was traded to the Boston Red Sox for outfielder Lou Clinton. For the Angels and Bosox combined for 1964, Thomas finished with 15 home runs and 66 RBIs. He had a strong season for Boston in 1965, hitting 27 doubles and 22 home runs with 75 RBIs and a .271 batting average. It was his last season as a full-time major league player. From 1966 through 1968, Thomas was a part-time performer for the Atlanta Braves, Chicago Cubs and Houston Astros, before finishing his playing career in Japan. Thomas was an All-Star in 1962.

Ted Williams

The arrival of the 1960s brought with it the end of the magnificent career of Ted Williams. His twenty-first – and last – season was 1960, and he left the game as dramatically as he had entered it in 1939.

In his 2-plus decades as a major leaguer, Williams won 6 batting titles and 2 Triple Crowns to go with 2 Most Valuable Player awards. He remains the last player to hit over .400, having batted .406 in 1941.

Williams entered the 1960 campaign with a career batting average of .346 with 492 home runs. Injuries limited him to only 6 hits and 20 at-bats through May, but he hit .329 with 11 home runs and 24 RBIs in June. He became only the fourth player in major league history to hit 500 career home runs, and would pass New York Giants great Mel Ott for the number 3 all-time position by the end of the season, trailing only Babe Ruth and Jimmy Foxx at the time he retired. Williams batted .315 in July and .313 in August.

Ted Williams played his last major league game in front of 10,454 Bosox fans at Fenway Park on September 28, 1960. In his final game, Williams walked in his first plate appearance, eventually scoring on Lou Clinton's sacrifice fly. In the third inning he flied out to Jackie Brandt in center field. In the fifth inning, he flied out to right fielder Al Pilarcik.

When Williams came to bat with one out in the bottom of the eighth, the Orioles were leading 4-2. Jack Fisher had replaced Orioles starter Steve Barber after only one out in the first inning, and had shut out the Red Sox in relief, including Williams in his previous 2 at-bats. Everyone in the stadium knew that this would probably be the last time they would see Williams hit in Fenway Park, and hit he did. In his last major league at-bat, Williams took a Fisher fast ball to deep center field for his career home run number 521. After circling the bases, Williams acknowledged the standing ovation and disappeared into the Red Sox dugout for the last time. Carroll Hardy replaced him in left field in the top of the ninth.

Williams' home run cut the Orioles lead to 4-3. Mike Fornieles retired the Orioles in order in the top of the ninth, and Boston rallied for 2 more runs in the bottom of the ninth off Fisher.

Williams hit .316 that last season, with 29 home runs and 72 RBIs for a Boston team that would finish seventh in the American League, 32 games behind the New York Yankees. As bad as the Red Sox might have been in 1960, they still managed to send Teddy Ball home a winner.

Carl Yastrzemski

It must be nice to be able to replace one Hall of Fame outfielder with another one. The Yankees did that when Joe DiMaggio relinquished center field to Mickey Mantle. And the Red Sox followed suit a decade later, replacing the great Ted Williams, who retired at the end of the 1960 season, with a pure hitter named Carl Yastrzemski.

Yaz was the prototype for the complete ballplayer, hitting for power and average and playing left field superbly throughout his 23 major league seasons, all with the Red Sox. Signed as a free agent in 1958, he debuted in left field for the Red Sox in 1961. He batted .266 as a rookie, driving in 80 runs. The next year he raised his batting average to .296, with 19 home runs and 94 RBIs. His offensive numbers would only get better.

In 1963, Yastrzemski hit .321 to win his first American League batting championship. That year, he also led the league in hits (183), doubles (40) and bases on balls (95). He continued hitting well over the next three years, leading the league in doubles in 1965 and 1966. He failed to repeat as doubles leader in 1967, but he compensated in other ways.

1967 was a miracle season for Yastrzemski and for the Red Sox. The team won the American League pennant by one game in a three-team race that came down to the last day of the season. Yaz almost single-handedly carried the Red Sox to the pennant. In the last 12 games of the season, he hit 5 home runs, scored 14 runs and drove in

16 runs. In the last two "must win" games against the Minnesota Twins, Yastrzemski went 7 for 8 with 6 RBIs.

When the regular season had ended, Yastrzemski was at the top of the league in nearly every offensive category: hits (189), runs (112), home runs (44, tied with Minnesota's Harmon Killebrew), RBIs (121), total bases (360), and slugging percentage (.622) as well as batting average (.326 for his second batting title). His Triple Crown leadership in home runs, RBIs and batting average earned Yaz the league's Most Valuable Player award. During the 1967 World Series, which the St. Louis Cardinals won in 7 games, Yastrzemski continued his offensive onslaught, batting .400 with 3 home runs.

In 1968, Yastrzemski won his third batting title with a .301 average, the league's only .300 hitter that year and the lowest average ever for a batting champion. He closed out the 1960s with another superb year in 1969, hitting 40 home runs and driving in 111 runs, though he hit only .255. He won the Gold Glove for his consistent excellence in left field 5 times during the 1960s, and 6 times in all during his career.

Yastrzemski retired with 3,419 major league hits, ranking seventh all time in that category. He also hit over 400 home runs with more than 1,800 lifetime RBIs. The 1968 Triple Crown winner was voted into the Baseball Hall of Fame in 1989.

Red Sox League Leaders & Awards

Batting Average:

1960, Pete Runnels, .320

1962, Pete Runnels, .326

1963, Carl Yastrzemski, .321

1967, Carl Yastrzemski, .326

1968, Carl Yastrzemski, .301

Home Runs:

1965, Tony Conigliaro, 32

1967, Carl Yastrzemski, 44

Runs Batted In:

1963, Dick Stuart, 118

1967, Carl Yastrzemski, 121

1968, Ken Harrelson, 109

Carl Yastrzemski
3-Time Batting Champion
in the 1960s and Triple
Crown Winner in 1967

Wins:

1967, Jim Lonborg, 22

Strikeouts:

1967, Jim Lonborg, 246

Most Valuable Player:

Carl Yastrzemski, 1967

Cy Young:

Jim Lonborg, 1967

Rookie of the Year:

Don Schwall, 1961

Gold Gloves

First Base:

George Scott, 1967-1968

Outfield:

Carl Yastrzemski, 1963, 1965, 1967-1969

Reggie Smith, 1968

Don Schwall

A 15-game winner, Schwall was American League Rookie of the Year in 1961.

The Catchers

Joe Azcue

In a major league career that spanned the 1960s, Joe Azcue was known as a dependable catcher with a strong, accurate throwing arm. He led American League catchers in fielding percentage in 1967 and 1968. Over his 11-year career, he threw out more than 45 percent of base runners attempting to steal, and in 1966 he threw out 62 percent. And, on occasion, he could hit.

A Cuban native, Azcue was signed by the Cincinnati Reds in 1956 and appeared in 14 games with the Reds at the end of the 1960 season, hitting .097. He was purchased by the Milwaukee Braves and returned to the minors for the 1961 season, and in December of 1961 was traded with Ed Charles and Manny Jimenez to the Kansas City Athletics for Lou Klimchock and Bob Shaw. He hit .229 as the Athletics' backup catcher, and at the beginning of the 1963 season was traded with Dick Howser to the Cleveland Indians for Doc Edwards.

Azcue had his best seasons, as a hitter and defensively, with the Indians. He hit .284 with the Tribe in 1963 with career highs in home runs (14) and RBIs (46). He hit .273 in 1964 and .230 in 1965, and then bounced back to hit .275 in 1966 and .280 in 1968.

In April of 1969, Azcue was part of a blockbuster deal with the Boston Red Sox. Cleveland sent Azcue, Vicente Romo and Sonny

Siebert to Boston for Ken Harrelson, Dick Ellsworth and Juan Pizarro. Azcue appeared in only 19 games for the Red Sox, hitting .216, and then was traded to the California Angels for Tom Satriano. He finished the 1969 season with a combined .223 batting average, and then hit .242 for California in 1970, his last full season in the majors. Azcue sat out the 1971 season, and then played a total of 14 games for the Angels and the Milwaukee Brewers in 1972 before retiring.

In 11 big league seasons, Azcue collected 712 hits for a .252 career batting average.

Joe Azcue

Came to Boston in the trade that sent Ken Harrelson to Cleveland, then was traded 19 games later to the California Angels.

Elston Howard

The career of Elston Howard belonged to a gentleman who was both a great ballplayer and a true pioneer in so many aspects of the modern game.

A standout athlete in high school, Howard turned down college football scholarships to play for the Kansas City Monarchs starting in 1948. He was signed by the New York Yankees in 1950, and made his first appearance with the Yankees in 1955, the first African American to play in a Yankee uniform. (He also got a hit in his first at-bat for the Yankees.)

For the next 5 years Howard played fill-in roles at catcher, first base and in the outfield for Yankee teams loaded with talent. By 1961, he had become the Yankees' regular catcher, hitting .348 that year with 21 home runs and 77 RBIs. In 1962, he drove in a career-high 91 runs, and in 1963, Howard hit 28 home runs with 85 RBIs to win the American League Most Valuable Player award, the first African American to do so.

Howard's defense was as solid as his hitting, and he won the Gold Glove for catching in 1963 and 1964. Howard was also an excellent handler of pitchers. In his 13 seasons with the Yankees, Howard was chosen for the American League All-Star team 9 times.

Howard appeared in 54 World Series games, the third highest total in major league history behind only Yankee teammates Yogi Berra and Mickey Mantle. (Another first: Howard homered in his debut World Series at-bat.) The last 7 World Series appearances were with the Boston Red Sox, where Howard played a critical in the Bosox' pennant-winning re-emergence after being dealt to Boston midway through the 1967 season. He retired after the 1968 season.

Elston Howard

Nine times an All-Star, Howard batted .272 over his 14-year major league career with the Yankees and the Red Sox.

Russ Nixon

Russ Nixon was a major league catcher for 12 seasons (and a scout, coach and manager for 45 more). In those 12 seasons, he set only one record, but it remains a record as unlikely to be broken as any in baseball.

Nixon was signed by the Cleveland Indians in 1953 and made his major league debut in 1957, hitting .281 in 62 games. In 1958, he

batted .301 for Cleveland with 9 home runs and 46 RBIs. After batting .240 in 1959, Cleveland traded Nixon with Carroll Hardy to the Boston Red Sox for Ted Bowsfield and Marty Keough.

Nixon spent the next 6 seasons in a Red Sox uniform, batting .298 in 1960 and .289 in 1961. But in each season in Boston, Nixon played only a part-time role, splitting the team's catching duties with the likes of Haywood Sullivan, Jim Pagliaroni and Bob Tillman. At the opening of the 1966 season, Nixon was traded with Chuck Schilling to the Minnesota Twins for pitcher Dick Stigman and a player to be named later. He batted .260 for the Twins in 1966, mostly as a pinch hitter, and hit .235 in 1967, strictly in a reserve role. He returned to the Red Sox in 1968 after being released by the Twins, batting .153 in only 29 games. At the end of the season, he was acquired by the Chicago White Sox, but retired before ever playing for Chicago.

In 12 seasons in the majors, Nixon collected 670 hits for a .268 career batting average. He hit a total of 27 home runs with 266 runs batted in. And his only offensive career record was for something he never did. Russ Nixon played in more games (906) than any other major league player ... who never stole a base.

Gene Oliver

Gene Oliver had a consistently productive 10-year career in the major leagues, but his value was recognized mostly as a backup catcher. In only 2 seasons did he have the opportunity to play full-time, and when he got that opportunity, he delivered.

Oliver was attending Northwestern University when he signed with the St. Louis Cardinals in 1956. After 3 years in the Cardinals' farm system, Oliver was called up and appeared in 68 games for St. Louis, playing catcher, first base and in the outfield. He batted .244 with 6 home runs and 28 RBIs, only to find himself back in the minors for the next 2 seasons. He assured his ticket back to the major leagues by hitting .302 in 1961 at the Triple-A level, with 36 home runs and 100 runs batted in.

Oliver had power and, for a catcher, pretty good speed on the base paths. He hit .258 for the Cardinals in 1962 with 14 home runs and 45 RBIs, and opened the 1963 season in St. Louis when he was traded with Bob Sadowski to the Milwaukee Braves for Lew Burdette. He hit 17 homes runs with 65 RBIs in 1963, and batted .276 in 1964 with 13 home runs and 49 RBIs. He hit a career-best 21 home runs in 1965.

In 1967, he was traded to the Philadelphia Phillies for catcher Bob Uecker. After batting .224 as the Phillies' everyday catcher, he was traded again with Dick Ellsworth to the Boston Red Sox for Mike Ryan and cash. Over the next 2 seasons, Oliver appeared in only 47 games combined for the Red Sox and the Chicago Cubs. He was released by the Cubs near the end of the 1969 season.

Oliver ended his 10-year career with a .246 batting average on 546 hits and 93 home runs.

Jim Pagliaroni

Jim Pagliaroni was strictly a 1960s catcher. All but one game of his decade-long career was played in the 1960s, where he toiled for 4 teams with defensive prowess, occasional pop in his bat, and a cool head that helped 2 pitchers toss no-hitters, and one do so perfectly.

Pagliaroni was signed by the Boston Red Sox in 1955. He appeared in one game that season, and didn't reappear in the major leagues until he was brought up from the minors for 28 games in 1960. In 1961 Pagliaroni appeared in 120 games, more than any other Red Sox catcher, and posted a .242 batting average with 16 home runs and 58 runs batted in. In 1962, he batted .258 with 11 home runs and 37 RBIs, and caught his first no-hitter, pitched by Bill Monbouquette against the Chicago White Sox.

In the off-season, Pagliaroni was traded with pitcher Don Schwall to the Pittsburgh Pirates for Jack Lamabe and Dick Stuart. He started the 1963 season as the backup to the Pirates' regular catcher, Smokey Burgess, but when Burgess was sidelined by injury, Pagliaroni stepped into an everyday playing role, batting .239 with 11 home runs and 26 RBIs. His best season in Pittsburgh came in 1965, when he batted .268 with 17 home runs and 65 runs batted in. In his 5 seasons in Pittsburgh, Pagliaroni hits a combined .254 and averaged 10 home runs and 37 RBIs per season.

In December of 1967, Pagliaroni was purchased by the Oakland Athletics. He played in 66 games, including the perfect game hurled by Jim "Catfish" Hunter. He batted .246 with 6 home runs and 20 RBIs for the Athletics.

Pagliaroni split the 1969 season between Oakland and the Seattle Pilots, batting a combined .241 in 54 games. He retired at age 31 after the 1969 season.

Pagliaroni finished his major league career with 622 hit and a .252 batting average. He led all National League catchers in fielding percentage in 1966.

Jim Pagliaroni

In 1961, Pagliaroni hit the game-winning,
bottom-of-the-ninth home run in both ends of a
double header ... one a grand slam.

Mike Ryan

Mike Ryan was a major league catcher for 11 seasons and 3 teams, starting in 1964 with the Boston Red Sox. He never hit for a batting average higher than .214 for the Red Sox and was traded in 1967 to the Philadelphia Phillies for Dick Ellsworth and Gene Oliver.

Ryan played 6 years with the Phillies, hitting .190 combined, and played in 15 games for the Pittsburgh Pirates in 1974 before retiring with a .193 career batting average.

Bob Tillman

Bob Tillman signed with the Boston Red Sox in 1958 and made his major league debut in 1962, batting .229 in his rookie season. His best season in Boston came in 1964, when he batted .278 with 17 home runs and 61 RBIs.

Tillman was sold to the New York Yankees in 1967, and then spent 3 seasons with the Atlanta Braves prior to retiring after the 1970 season. A solid defensive catcher, Tillman lasted 9 seasons in the major leagues with 540 hits and a career .232 batting average.

Red Sox Team Leaders of the 1960s

Batting Average:

.326, Carl Yastrzemski, 1967

.326, Pete Runnels, 1962

.321, Carl Yastrzemski, 1963

.320, Pete Runnels, 1960

.317, Pete Runnels, 1961

Home Runs:

44, Carl Yastrzemski, 1967

42, Dick Stuart, 1963

40, Carl Yastrzemski, 1969

40, Rico Petrocelli, 1969

35, Ken Harrelson, 1968

Pete Runnels

Runs Batted In:

121, Carl Yastrzemski, 1967

118, Dick Stuart, 1963

114, Dick Stuart, 1964

111, Carl Yastrzemski, 1969

109, Ken Harrelson, 1968

Wins:

22, Jim Lonborg, 1967

20, Bill Monbouquette, 1963

17, Ray Culp, 1969

16, Ray Culp, 1968

16, Dick Ellsworth, 1968

16, Dick Radatz, 1964

Bill Monbouquette

Strikeouts:

246, Jim Lonborg, 1967

190, Ray Culp, 1968

181, Dick Radatz, 1964

174, Bill Monbouquette, 1963

172, Ray Culp, 1969

Dick Radatz

Earned Run Average:

2.77, Lee Stange, 1967

2.91, Ray Culp, 1968

3.03, Dick Ellsworth, 1968

3.11, Mike Nagy, 1969

3.12, Gary Bell, 1968

Lee Stange

The Pitchers

Gary Bell

Gary Bell started out his career as a hard-throwing starter, relying on heat and guts while pitching for struggling Cleveland Indians teams. He gradually evolved into one of the American League's most effective middle relievers with off-speed pitches that helped him get more out of less fastball.

Bell was signed by the Indians and was pitching in the majors 3 years later, going 12-10 with a 3.31 ERA as an Indians starter. In 1959, again as mostly a starter for the Tribe, Bell went 16-11 with a 4.04 ERA

His record slipped to 9-10 in 1960 and 12-16 in 1961. In 1962, he was moved back to the Indians bullpen, going 10-9 with 12 saves. During the next 3 seasons, working almost exclusively in relief, Bell went 22-16 with a combined 3.42 ERA. That year produced career highs in both appearances (60) and saves (17). In 1966, Bell returned to the Indians' starting rotation, posting a 14-15 record with a 3.22 ERA. He led the Indians pitching staff in games started (37), complete games (12), and finished fifth in the American League (and second on the team to league leader Sam McDowell) with a career-best 194 strikeouts.

Bell started the 1967 season as a starter and lost 5 of his first 6 decisions for Cleveland before being traded to the Boston Red Sox for Tony Horton and Don Demeter. He went 12-8 the rest of the way for the pennant-winning Bosox, and followed up with an 11-11 season for Boston in 1968.

The Seattle Pilots selected Bell in the expansion draft prior to the 1969 season, and he went 2-6 for Seattle before being traded to the Chicago White Sox for pitcher Bob Locker. He appeared in 23 games for the White Sox with no decisions before being released and retiring. He ended his career with a 121-117 record with a 3.68 ERA over 12 seasons. He was a 3-time All-Star: in 1960, 1966 and 1968.

Gary Bell

Won 12 games down the
pennant stretch for the
Red Sox in 1967.

Dennis Bennett

Left-hander Dennis Bennett pitched for 4 different major league teams in a 7-year career. He signed with the Philadelphia Phillies in 1958 and made his major league debut with the team in 1962, going 9-9 with a 3.81 ERA as a rookie with 2 shutouts and 3 saves.

Bennett's best season in Philadelphia came in 1964 when he was 12-14 with a 3.68 earned run average in 208 innings pitched. In November of 1964 he was traded to the Boston Red Sox for first baseman Dick Stuart. Hampered by arm problems, he was 12-13 in 3 seasons with Boston. He also pitched with the New York Mets and California Angels before retiring after the 1968 season. Bennett's career record was 43-47 with a 3.69 ERA.

Ted Bowsfield

Ted Bowsfield was a sinkerball southpaw who pitched for 4 different teams during a 7-year major league career. Early in his career, he was described by New York Yankees manager Casey Stengel as "that fella that throws them ground balls." And he was that fella.

Bowsfield was signed by the Boston Red Sox in 1954 and made his big league debut with Boston in 1958, going 4-2 with a 3.84 ERA in 16

appearances that season. He made the majors to stay in 1960, splitting a 4-6 season between Boston and the Cleveland Indians after being traded with Marty Keough for Carroll Hardy and Russ Nixon.

After the 1960 season, Bowsfield was selected by the Los Angeles Angels in the 1960 expansion draft. After working mostly out of the bullpen during his first 3 major league seasons, Bowsfield moved immediately into the Angels' starting rotation and had the best season of his career, going 11-8 with a 3.73 ERA for the fledgling Angels. He followed up in 1962 with a 9-8 record and a 4.40 ERA, and then was dealt to the Kansas City Athletics to complete an earlier deal for pitcher Dan Orsinski.

In 2 seasons with Kansas City, Bowsfield pitched mostly out of the bullpen, going a combined 9-14 with a 4.27 ERA. He retired at the close of the 1964 season at age 29.

In 7 major league seasons, Bowsfield posted a combined record of 37-39 with a 4.35 ERA.

Galen Cisco

Galen Cisco was signed by the Boston Red Sox in 1958 after being a 2-sport star with the Ohio State University. He made his major league debut with Boston in 1961, going 2-4 with a 6.71 ERA.

Cisco was acquired by the New York Mets toward the end of the 1962 season, and was a starter-reliever for the Mets, going 7-15 in 1963 and 6-19 in 1964. His earned run average in 1964 was only 3.62, with a pair of shutouts. He retired after the 1969 season with a 25-56 career record and a 4.56 ERA.

Gene Conley

Gene Conley was the first athlete to play for World Champions in two major different sports: for the Milwaukee Braves as a pitcher in 1957, and as a member of the NBA's Boston Celtics from 1959 to 1962.

A 2-sport All-American at Washington State University, the 6-foot-eight-inch Conley was signed by the Boston Braves in 1951. He was outstanding from the start of his professional baseball career, winning 20 games his first season, and then going 11-4 for Milwaukee in the American Association before being called up to Boston at the end of the 1952 season, and promptly losing his first 3 major league starts. He spent the 1953 season in the minors, winning 23 games at the Triple-A level.

In 1954 he stepped right into the Braves' starting rotation, and was 14-9 in his rookie season, with a 2.96 ERA, fifth best in the National League. Conley was named to the All-Star team, and finished third in the voting for Rookie of the Year, won in 1954 by Wally Moon (Ernie Banks finished second ... and Hank Aaron fourth).

Conley was 11-7 in 1955, and then didn't win more than 9 games in a season until 1959 when, as a member of the Philadelphia Phillies, he went 12-7 with a 3.00 earned run average. He was 8-14 for the Phillies in 1960, and then was traded to the Boston Red Sox for Frank Sullivan. He was 11-14 for the Red Sox in 1961, finishing third on the team in victories behind Don Schwall and Bill Monbouquette. In 1962, his 15-14 record tied him with Monbouquette for the team lead in wins.

Conley appeared in 9 games for Boston in 1963, going 3-4 with an ERA of 6.64. He was released by the Red Sox and signed the next day with the Cleveland Indians, but never pitched in an Indians' uniform, retiring in June at age 32.

In 11 major league seasons, Conley posted a 91-96 record with a career ERA of 3.82. He struck out 888 batters and pitched 13 shutouts.

Ray Culp

Ray Culp was a strapping Texan who threw hard and won often. In fact, from 1963 through 1970, the right-hander had only a single losing season – his only season as a member of the Chicago Cubs.

Culp was signed by the Philadelphia Phillies in 1959 and worked his way through the Phillies' farm system to make the big league club as a member of the starting rotation in 1963. He was 14-11 as a rookie with a 2.97 ERA, pitching 203.1 innings with 10 complete games and 5 shutouts. He was selected that year as *The Sporting News* National League Rookie Pitcher of the Year and was a member of the National League All-Star team.

He was 8-7 in 1964 and followed in 1965 with a 14-10 record and a 3.22 ERA, third on the team in victories behind Jim Bunning and Chris Short. He moved to the bullpen in 1966, going 7-4 with a 5.04 ERA, and then was traded to the Chicago Cubs for Dick Ellsworth.

Culp went 8-11 for the Cubs in 1967, and then was acquired by the Boston Red Sox, where his career took off to reflect the promise he showed in his rookie season. Culp was 16-6 for Boston in 1968 with a 2.91 ERA. He pitched 11 complete games for the Red Sox with 6 shutouts.

Culp followed up in 1969 with a 17-8 season and a 3.81 ERA. He also earned a spot on the American league All-Star team that season. Culp was 17-14 for Boston in 1970 with a 3.04 ERA and 15 complete games in 33 starts. He was fifth in the league in strikeouts with 197. It was his last winning season.

Culp's record slipped to 14-16 in 1971 with a 3.60 ERA, but by this time his arm was effectively pitched out. He was 5-8 for Boston in 1972, and made only 10 appearances in 1973, going 2-6. He was released by the Red Sox following the 1973 season, and retired at age 31. Culp finished with a career record of 122-101 and a 3.58 ERA.

Ike Delock

Ike Delock pitched for the Boston Red Sox for 11 seasons, starting in 1952. His best season with the Red Sox came in 1958, when he was 14-8 with a 3.38 ERA. He followed up in 1959 with an 11-6 season and a 2.95 ERA.

In the 1960s, Delock worked out of the Red Sox starting rotation, going 9-10 in 1960 and 6-9 in 1961. In 1963, he was released by the Red Sox and signed with the Baltimore Orioles. He went 1-3 for the Orioles before being released. He retired with a career record of 84-75 with a 4.03 ERA.

Dick Ellsworth

Dick Ellsworth was a dependable starter for the Chicago Cubs and 4 other major league teams from 1960 through 1971. He is one of the few pitchers in major league history to follow a 20-loss season with a 20-victory campaign.

Ellsworth was signed by the Cubs in 1958 out of Fresno High School, where his teammates included future major league pitcher Jim Maloney. Ellsworth made the Cubs' roster for keeps in 1960. From 1960 through 1966, he averaged 34 starts and 234 innings per season for Chicago. Although his ERA for that period was a respectable 3.68, his won-loss record for less-than-respectable Cubs teams was only 84-109.

After going 9-20 in 1962, Ellsworth posted a 22-10 record for 1963. His 2.11 ERA that season was second in the league only to the 1.88 for Sandy Koufax. But he would never match the success of 1963 again as a Cubs starter. He won 14 games in both 1964 and 1965, and led the National League in losses in 1966 (8-20).

Ellsworth was traded to Philadelphia for pitcher Ray Culp, and went 6-7 in his only season with the Phillies. He was traded to the Boston Red Sox and went 16-7 in 1968. He was 9-12 for the Cleveland Indians over the next 2 seasons, and retired in 1971 after a short stay with the Milwaukee Brewers. Ellsworth's career record was 115-137 with a 3.72 ERA. He was an All-Star in 1964

Mike Fornieles

Mike Fornieles was signed by the Washington Senators in 1950 and made his major league debut with that team in 1952, pitching a 5-0 1-hitter against the Philadelphia Athletics. He was traded to the Chicago White Sox in 1952, to the Baltimore Orioles in 1956 and to the Boston Red Sox in 1957.

Fornieles remained in Boston for 7 seasons, working primarily as a reliever. His best season came in 1960 when Fornieles was 10-5 with a 2.64 ERA. His 70 appearances and 48 games finished both led the American League, as did his 14 saves.

Fornieles was 9-8 with 15 saves for Boston in 1961. He pitched for the Minnesota Twins in 1963 and then retired after a 12-year major league career. He posted a career record of 63-64 with a 3.96 ERA.

Ron Kline

Ron Kline's career as a major league pitcher spanned 17 seasons and 9 teams. He started his career as a starting pitcher, with mixed results, and experienced his best seasons after the age of 30, when he emerged as one of the American League's most effective and durable relievers ... yet is hardly counted today among the premier relievers of the 1960s despite putting up numbers that say he deserves that kind of accolade.

Kline was signed by the Pittsburgh Pirates in 1950 and made his major league debut in 1952, going 0-7 out of the Pirates' bullpen that year. He spent the next 2 years in military service, and returned to the Pirates in 1955, going 6-13 as a starter and reliever. In 1956 he worked out of the Pirates' starting rotation, making 39 starts and pitching 264 innings on his way to a 14-18 record and a 3.38 ERA. He won 9 and 13 games in each of the next 2 seasons respectively, while losing 16 decisions both years. After an 11-13 season with Pittsburgh in 1959, he was traded to the St. Louis Cardinals for Tom Cheney and Gino Cimoli.

Kline was 4-9 in 1960, his only season with the Cardinals. He was purchased by the Los Angeles Dodgers in 1961, and was 8-9 that year, which he finished with the Detroit Tigers. After a 3-6 season with the Tigers in 1962, he was purchased by the Washington Senators.

It would be a career-lifting move for the 31-year-old right-hander, who had been 68-107 to this point as a starter and reliever. For the

Senators, he would move to the bullpen and never move out. His numbers as a relief specialist revealed why.

For the Senators in 1963, Kline was 3-8 with a 2.79 ERA. He finished 46 of his 62 appearances and saved 17 games for a team that won only 56 on the season. He followed up in 1964 with a 10-7 season and a 2.32 ERA, appearing in 61 games and finishing 52 of them, with 14 saves.

In 1965, Kline led the American League with 29 saves, going 7-6 with a 2.63 ERA. In 1966, he tallied 23 saves with a record of 6-4 and a 2.39 earned run average. In the off season, Kline was traded by the Senators to the Minnesota Twins for Bernie Allen and Camilo Pascual. He was 7-1 for the Twins in 1967 with a 3.77 ERA, and was traded after only one season with the Twins to the Pirates for catcher Bob Oliver. Kline was 12-5 for the Pirates in 1968 with a 1.68 ERA.

He spent the 1969 season with 3 teams: the Pirates, the San Francisco Giants (traded for Joe Gibbon) and the Boston Red Sox. For the season, he was a combined 1-5 in 43 relief appearances. He signed with Atlanta for the 1970 season, but retired after only 5 appearances with the Braves.

In his prime, from 1963 through 1968, Kline appeared in 370 games (an average of 62 per season) with 45 victories, 95 saves and a combined ERA of 2.52. Kline finished with a career record of 114-144 and a 3.75 ERA.

Jack Lamabe

Jack Lamabe was a right-handed relief specialist who pitched for 7 different teams during his 7-year major league career.

Lamabe signed with the Philadelphia Phillies in 1956 but ultimately made it to the big leagues in 1962 with the Pittsburgh Pirates, going 3-1 with a 2.88 ERA and 2 saves. He was traded the next winter with Dick Stuart to the Boston Red Sox for Jim Pagliaroni and Don Schwall.

This "one and out" pattern would continue throughout most of Lamabe's career, making stops with the Houston Astros, Chicago White Sox, New York Mets, St. Louis Cardinals and Chicago Cubs. His best season came in 1964 with Boston. Lamabe appeared in 65 games and went 7-4 with a 3.15 ERA and 6 saves. For his career, Lamabe compiled a record of 33-41 with 15 saves and a 4.24 earned run average.

Jim Lonborg

From 1901 to 1908, the incomparable Cy Young won 192 games for the Boston Red Sox. In 1967, the second coming of Cy Young in a Boston uniform arrived in the form of another right-hander named Jim Lonborg.

Lonborg was signed by the Red Sox in 1963 off the campus of Stanford University. He was a regular starter for Boston during his rookie season in 1965, going 9-17 for the ninth-place Red Sox. His record improved to 10-10 in 1966, and then came his "Cy Young" season of 1967.

After years of toiling in the second division, the Red Sox won the 1967 American League pennant in one of the most exciting stretch drives ever. The Boston pennant was earned on the exploits of Carl Yastrzemski's Triple Crown bat and Lonborg's outstanding pitching: 22-9 with 3.16 ERA and a league-leading 246 strikeouts. Lonborg was voted the American League Cy Young award that year, the first year that the award was made for the best pitcher in each league.

Lonborg never had a season like that again for the Red Sox. From 1968 to 1971, Lonborg was 27-29 for the Red Sox, and was then swapped to the Milwaukee Brewers in a 10-player deal. He was 14-12 for the Brewers in 1972 with a career-best 2.83 ERA, and then was traded to the Philadelphia Phillies. He had his some of his best post-Cy Young seasons with Philadelphia, going 17-13 in 1974 and 18-10 in 1976. For his 15-season career, Lonborg posted a 157-137 record with a combined 3.86 ERA.

Don McMahon

Relief pitcher may be the most expendable position on a major league ball club. With a few exceptions (such as Hoyt Wilhelm, Roy Face and Lindy McDaniel), most relievers cannot extend top performance season after season.

Don McMahon was one of those exceptions, a standout reliever for 7 different clubs over an 18-year career. Only once did he lead the league in any pitching category, but you could count on his durable arm and pitching savvy for a full season of putting out fires.

McMahon was signed by the Boston Braves in 1950. His major league debut was delayed by military service and 5 years of minor league seasoning. But when he finally made it to the Braves, he did it in a big way: Appearing in 32 games for the 1957 World Series champions, McMahon went 2-3 with a 1.54 ERA and 9 saves. In 1958, he was selected for the National League All-Star team on the way to a 7-2 season with 8 saves. In 1959, he led the league in games finished (49) and saves (15) with a 5-3 record and 2.57 ERA.

McMahon spent 6 seasons with the Braves, appearing in 233 games and tallying 50 saves with a combined ERA of 3.34. In May of 1962, he was purchased by the Houston Colt .45s, where he toiled for 2 seasons (6-10 with 13 saves and a 2.81 ERA) before being purchased by the Cleveland Indians. In 3 years with the Tribe, McMahon appeared in 140 games, posting a combined record of 10-8 with 28 saves and a 2.81 ERA.

In June of 1966, the Indians traded McMahon and pitcher Lee Stange to the Boston Red Sox for Dick Radatz. Again he was effective (11 saves and a 2.82 ERA in 60 appearances) and again he was traded, this time to the Chicago White Sox for infielder Jerry Adair. McMahon spent a "split" season with the White Sox in 1967-1968, going a combined 7-1 with a 1.77 ERA in 77 appearances.

He was then traded to the Detroit Tigers (for pitcher Dennis Ribant), where he appeared in 54 games over parts of 2 seasons, going 6-6 with 12 saves and a 2.97 ERA.

In August of 1969, McMahon was dealt to the San Francisco Giants. He followed with 2 of the best seasons of his career. He appeared in 61 games both seasons, going 9-5 with 19 saves and a 2.96 ERA in 1970, and 10-6 in 1971 with 4 saves. But the juice finally began to fade from his arm. McMahon appeared in only 44 games in 1972 and only 22 in 1973. He was released by the Giants during the 1974 season.

McMahon finished his career at 90-68 with a 2.96 ERA. At the time he retired, his 874 career appearances (all but 2 in relief) were the fourth most all-time after Wilhelm, McDaniel and Cy Young.

Bill Monbouquette

Bill Monbouquette was clearly the best starting pitcher in the Boston Red Sox rotation when the Red Sox were at their worst: during the first half of the 1960s. Then, as Red Sox fortunes turned suddenly to produce a pennant in 1967, Monbouquette had faded into the pitched-out twilight of his too-brief career, and had moved on to other teams.

A Medford, Massachusetts native, the local boy signed with the Red Sox in 1955 and made his first big league appearance in 1958. He went 7-7 for the Red Sox in 1959, starting in half of his 34 appearances.

By 1960, Monbouquette was a regular in Boston's starting rotation, going 14-11 with a 3.64 ERA. His 14 victories were second-highest on the Red Sox staff (to Don Schwall's 15-7 record), and Monbouquette led the team in games started (32), innings pitched (236.1) and strikeouts (161). In 1961 and 1962, he won 14 and 15 games, respectively. He pitched 4 shutouts in 1962 and posted a 3.33 ERA, his best in Boston.

In 1963 Monbouquette emerged as the undisputed ace of the Boston staff. That season he went 20-10 with a 3.81 ERA. He recorded career highs in innings pitched (266.2) and strikeouts (174). It was his last winning season in Boston. His record fell to 13-14 in 1964 and to 10-18 in 1965. His 18 losses were the most by any American League pitcher that season, and were "earned" despite a very respectable

3.70 ERA. Following the 1965 season, the Red Sox traded Monbouquette to the Detroit Tigers for George Smith and George Thomas.

Monbouquete had little left for the Tigers, and struggled through a 7-8 season in 1966 that produced a 4.73 ERA. He split the 1967 season between the Tigers and the New York Yankees, going 6-5 with a 2.33 ERA. The 1968 season would be his last, split between the Yankees and the San Francisco Giants. Monbouquette went 5-8 with a combined 4.35 ERA.

Monbouquette pitched for 11 seasons in the major leagues, compiling a record of 114-111. He was a 3-time member of the American League All-Star team. He pitched a no-hitter against the Chicago White Sox in 1962.

Bill Monbouquette

Boston's ace from 1960-1963, winning 63
games, including a no-hitter.

Dave Morehead

Dave Morehead was signed by the Boston Red Sox in 1961 and was pitching in Boston's starting rotation 2 seasons later. As a rookie in 1963, Morehead went 10-13 with a 3.81 ERA in 29 starts that included 6 complete games and a shutout. In 1964, his record slipped to 8-15

with a 4.97 ERA, and in 1965, pitching for a ninth-place Red Sox team that lost 100 games, Morehead went 10-18 with a 4.06 ERA. His 18 defeats were the highest total in the American League.

Despite a losing record over his first 3 major league seasons, there were high expectations for him (in addition to both Bill Monbouquette and a young hurler named Jim Lonborg) as the pitching cornerstone of the Red Sox rebuilding efforts. It wasn't to be. Morehead suffered from arm injuries that limited him to 23 starts over the next 3 seasons, posting a combined record of 7-10 with a 3.70 ERA.

In 1968, the Kansas City Royals selected Morehead in the expansion draft, and he responded by going 2-3 with a 5.73 ERA in 21 appearances in 1969, all but 2 in relief. Morehead came back as a combination starter-reliever for Kansas City in 1970, going 3-5 with a 3.62 ERA. He retired after the 1970 season with a career record of 40-64 and a 4.15 ERA.

Chet Nichols

Left-hander Chet Nichols was a starter for the Braves and a reliever for the Red Sox. He made his major league debut with the Boston Braves in 1951, going 11-8 as a rookie starter and leading the National League with a 2.88 ERA. He next pitched with the Braves in Milwaukee, going 9-11 in 1954 and 9-8 in 1955.

Nichols was released by the Braves in 1958 and signed with the Boston Red Sox in 1959. His best season with Boston came in 1961 when he was 3-2 with a 2.09 ERA and 3 saves. Nichols finished his 9-year major league career at 34-36 with a 3.64 earned run average. He recorded 10 saves and 4 shutouts during his career.

Juan Pizarro

As a major league pitcher, lefty Juan Pizarro had two careers. For the first 9 years of his career, he was a starter (and occasional long reliever, as even ace starting pitchers saw occasional double duty in the 1960s). During the second half of his 18-year career, Pizarro was primarily a relief specialist, whose blazing fastball would no longer hold up for 9 innings but remained effective in spot relief situations, especially against left-handed batters.

Pizarro was signed by the Milwaukee Braves and was immediately a stand-out prospect in their minor league system, winning 23 games at Jacksonville in his first professional season. He spent the next 3 seasons pitching effectively in the Triple-A minors but had limited success as a starter-reliever for the Braves. From 1957 through 1960, Pizarro posted a combined record of 23-19 with a 3.93 ERA for Milwaukee.

In December of 1960, the Braves traded Pizarro and Joey Jay to the Cincinnati Reds for shortstop Roy McMillan. On the same day, the Reds sent Pizarro and Cal McLish to the Chicago White Sox for infielder Gene Freese. The trades that day were good for Cincinnati, as both Jay and Freese played critical roles in propelling the Reds to the 1961 National League pennant. The trades were also good for Pizarro, whose arrival in Chicago launched his career as a full-time – and highly successful – starter for the White Sox.

In 1961 for the White Sox, Pizarro achieved career highs in starts (25) and innings pitched (194.2). He struck out 188 batters on his way to a 14-7 season with a 3.05 ERA. After a 12-14 season in 1962, he followed up with 16-8 in 1963 (2.39 ERA) and 19-9 in 1964 (2.56 ERA). Pizarro and teammate Gary Peters (20-8 in 1964) were recognized as the two best left-handers in the American League. Pizarro was named to the American League All-Star team in both 1963 and 1964.

However, Pizarro's success was starting to take a toll on his arm. All those innings, all those strikeouts, all those fastballs led to arm miseries and diminished performance in 1965 (6-3) and 1966 (8-6). The White Sox traded Pizarro to the Pittsburgh Pirates as the player to be named later in the acquisitio0n of pitcher Wilbur Wood. Pizarro transitioned quickly to a relief role that meant more appearances – and fewer total innings – to take full advantage of his still explosive fastball.

From 1967 through 1974, Pizarro pitched for 6 different teams, going 33-39 with 20 saves in 206 appearances. His combined ERA for that period was 3.76. He retired after the 1974 season with a career record of 131-105.

Dick Radatz

During his relatively brief career, Dick Radatz more than any other pitcher in the 1960s redefined the emerging role of relief pitcher. His domineering presence on the pitching mound, as well as his blistering, almost unhittable fastball, ushered in the era of the relief specialist that has had such a profound impact on major league baseball in the second half of the twentieth century.

At 6-foot-5 and 235 pounds, Radatz was an imposing figure on the mound. He threw hard and with less than pinpoint accuracy, keeping hitters off balance and often swinging defensively at his heat. There was no finesse to his pitching style. He entered the game with one job: to blow the baseball past the hitter. For three years in the mid-1960s, no one did it better.

Radatz was signed by the Boston Red Sox out of Michigan State University in 1959. He made the big league club in 1962 and his impact was immediate. During his rookie season, the right-hander appeared in 62 games and finished 53 of them. He went 9-6 on a 2.24 earned run average. He struck out 144 batters in 124 innings pitched, and led the major leagues with 24 saves. He finished third in the voting for 1962 American League Rookie of the Year. (Yankee shortstop Tom Tresh was that year's winner.)

His dominance continued over the next 2 seasons. In 1963, Radatz finished 58 of the 66 games he appeared in, going 15-6 with a 1.97 ERA and 25 saves. That year he struck out 162 batters in only 132 innings, and finished fifth in the balloting for American League Most Valuable Player. In 1964, Radatz led the majors with 29 saves, finishing 67 games in 79 appearances, and posting a 16-9 record with a 2.29 ERA. He struck out 181 batters in 157 innings pitched.

Radatz never achieved those kinds of numbers again. As his fastball began to fade, so did his performance, going 9-11 in 1965 with a 3.91 ERA. Though he still recorded 22 saves in 1965, he struck out fewer batters (121) than innings pitched (124) for the first time in his career. He was winless in 1966, going 0-5 with a 4.64 ERA and only 14 saves in a season split between Boston and Cleveland. He hung on through 1969, making stops with the Chicago Cubs, Detroit Tigers and Montreal Expos. In the last 3 years of his career, Radatz was a combined 3-6 with only 8 saves.

Without that sizzling fastball, Radatz couldn't be effective. But when he had it, nearly every batter he faced became a strikeout waiting to happen.

Vicente Romo

Vicente Romo was a dominating pitcher in the Mexican League, winning over 180 games in a 16-year career. He pitched 8 seasons in the major leagues, as a reliever and sometimes starter, going 32-33 with a 3.36 earned run average and 52 saves for 5 different teams.

Romo made his debut with the Los Angeles Dodgers in 1968 and after one appearance was traded to the Cleveland Indians in 1968, going 5-3 for Cleveland with 12 saves and a 1.62 ERA. In 1969 he was traded with Joe Azcue and Sonny Siebert to the Boston Red Sox for Dick Ellsworth, Ken Harrelson and Juan Pizarro. He finished the season at 7-9 for Boston with a 3.18 ERA and was 7-3 for the Red Sox in 1970.

Over the next 4 seasons, split between the Chicago White Sox and the San Diego Padres, Romo was 11-15 with a 3.76 ERA. He played in Mexico from 1975 through 1981, and returned to the Dodgers in 1982 for 16 games, going 1-2 with a 3.03 earned run average.

Jose Santiago

Jose Santiago played a major role in the return to prominence by the Boston Red Sox in 1967. The right-handed Santiago was effective as both a starter and a reliever, leading the American League in winning percentage in 1967.

Santiago was signed by the Kansas City Athletics in 1959 and made his debut with the A's in 1963, picking up a relief victory in his first major league appearance. He was 0-6 for the A's in 1964, working primarily out of the Kansas City bullpen. He spent nearly all of the 1965 season back in the minor leagues, and then got his career break when the Red Sox purchased his contract prior to the 1966 season. Santiago made 28 starts (with 7 relief appearances) for Boston in 1966, going 12-13 with a 3.66 ERA.

His best season came in 1967. Again splitting his appearances between the starting rotation and middle relief, Santiago was 12-4 with a 3.59 earned run average. He was particularly effective down the stretch, going 8-0 after July 5. He was 5-0 in September with a 2.83 ERA and posted 2 complete games in 3 September starts.

Santiago pitched the opening game of the 1967 World Series, losing 2-1 to a Bob Gibson 6-hitter. In his first World Series at-bat, Santiago hit a solo home run off Gibson for Boston's only run that day. For the Series, Santiago was 0-2 with a 5.59 ERA.

Santiago worked strictly as a starter in 1968, going 9-4 with a 2.25 ERA by the All-Star break. He was named to the American League All-Star team. An elbow injury kept him from playing and effectively wiped out the rest of that season and, ultimately, his major league career. He appeared in only 10 games in 1969 and 8 more in 1970, with rehab stints in the minor leagues both seasons. But Santiago did not pitch again in the major leagues after July 1970. He retired with a 34-29 record and a 3.74 career ERA.

Don Schwall

At a time when the fortunes of the Boston Red Sox appeared to be dipping to their lowest, and following the farewell of the greatest of Red Sox hitters with the 1960 retirement of Ted Williams, Boston fans were pinning their hopes for Red Sox revival on 2 players who made their major league debuts in 1961. One of those players, Carl Yastrzemski, went on to become a Hall of Fame left fielder and Red Sox legend.

The other player, whose promise in 1961 seemed even greater than that of Yaz, was a right-handed pitcher named Don Schwall.

Schwall was signed by the Red Sox in 1958 off the campus of the University of Oklahoma, where he had won All-Big Eight basketball honors. He found immediate success moving through Boston's minor league system, winning 23 games in 1959 and 16 games with Minneapolis in the American Association in 1960.

Schwall started 1961 with Triple-A Seattle in the Pacific Coast League, going 3-1 before being called up to Boston. He made his major league debut on May 21, pitching 8 innings in a 4-1 win over the Chicago White Sox. Schwall won his first 5 decisions for the Red Sox, and was 11-2 when he pitched 3 scoreless innings in the 1961 All-Star game. Schwall finished the 1961 season at 15-7 with a 3.22 ERA and the American League Rookie of the Year award.

Schwall never again put up those kinds of numbers. He went 9-15 for the Red Sox in 1962, and that winter with traded with Jim Pagliaroni to the Pittsburgh Pirates for Jack Lamabe and Dick Stuart.

His best season in Pittsburgh came in 1965. Used primarily as a reliever, Schwall went 9-6 that season with a 2.92 ERA.

In 1966, Schwall was traded to the Atlanta Braves for Billy O'Dell. He appeared in 11 games for the Braves, going 3-3. He made one appearance for the Braves in 1967 and then retired at age 31. In 7 major league seasons, Schwall compiled a 49-48 record with a career ERA of 3.72.

Rollie Sheldon

Rollie Sheldon was signed by the New York Yankees in 1960 and made his major league debut in 1961, going 11-5 with a 3.60 ERA and 2 shutouts. Sheldon was 7-8 in 1962. He spent 1963 and most of 1964 with Richmond in the International League, going a combined 9-11

before being recalled to New York. He finished the 1964 season at 5-2 with the Yankees, posting a 3.61 ERA.

In 1965, Sheldon was traded to the Kansas City Athletics, going 10-8 with a 3.85 ERA. He was 5-13 for the A's and the Boston Red Sox in 1966, his last season in the major leagues. Sheldon finished his major league career at 38-36 with a 4.09 ERA.

Sonny Siebert

During the mid-1960s, the Cleveland Indians had not only the most prolific strikeout pitcher in Sam McDowell, but also the league's most lethal strikeout tandem. Sonny Siebert was the other half of that duo, and the right-handed complement to Sudden Sam.

Siebert was signed by the Indians out of the University of Missouri and pitched in Cleveland's farm system for 5 seasons. He was a .500 pitcher until 1962, when he won 15 games for Charleston in the Eastern League. After a 7-9 rookie season in 1964, Siebert moved into the Indians' starting rotation and stayed there for 4 seasons.

Cleveland's young starting rotation of McDowell, Siebert and Luis Tiant was one of the best in the American League in terms of "stuff." Unfortunately, that trio didn't have the supporting talent to turn them into consistent winners.

Of the 3, Siebert seems to fare best at first. In his first season as a full-time starter, Siebert went 16-8 with a 2.43 ERA and 191 strikeouts in 188.2 innings pitched. He finished the season fourth in the American League in strikeouts, second in strikeouts per 9 innings (9.11) and third in ERA. (Teammate McDowell led the league in all 3 categories.)

Siebert repeated his 16-8 campaign for 1966, increasing his innings pitched to 241 while keeping his ERA at a low 2.80. His 161 strikeouts were tenth best in the league (led again by McDowell). No other team in the American League had as potent a 1-2 strikeout punch.

Over the next 2 seasons, Siebert was a combined 22-22 for Cleveland despite a combined ERA of only 2.69. At the beginning of the 1969 season, Siebert was traded with Joe Azcue and Vicente Romo to the Boston Red Sox for Dick Ellsworth, Ken Harrelson and Juan Pizarro. He won 14 games for the Red Sox in 1969, 15 games in 1970, and 16 games in 1971.

After a 12-12 season in 1972, Siebert was traded to the Texas Rangers. He played for 4 different teams over the next 3 seasons, posting a combined 22-26. He retired after the 1975 season. During his 12-year career, Siebert won 140 games with a career ERA of 3.21.

Tracy Stallard

Tracy Stallard was a talented pitcher whose timing was not on par with his fastball. He spent most of his major league career with teams that couldn't provide the offensive or defensive support to convert his stuff into wins. He also happened to be the guy who was the opposing pitcher to Jim Bunning on June 21, 1964 – when Bunning pitched his perfect game.

And of course, Stallard was the man who delivered the pitch that Roger Maris sent into the stands on the last day of the 1961 season – the pitch that resulted in home run number 61, the pitch that would overshadow everything else in Stallard's career.

Stallard was signed out of high school by the Boston Red Sox in 1956. At 6-5 and 205 pounds, the lanky Stallard threw hard and, when he threw for strikes, was practically unhittable. He completed his entire high school career without being beaten, and pitched 2 no-hitters during his senior year.

Stallard spent 5 years in the Red Sox farm system, and made the big league club in 1961. He made 43 appearances that season, starting 14 games and finishing 10 games. He posted a 2-7 record with a 4.88 ERA. His last loss of the year was probably his best-pitched game, losing a 5-hitter by a score of 1-0. The only run Stallard allowed came off Maris' fourth-inning solo home run. It would be the only hit Maris would ever get off Stallard in 7 career at-bats.

Stallard spent the 1962 season in the minors, and after that season he was traded with Pumpsie Green to the New York Mets for Felix Mantilla. In New York, Stallard began the season in the bullpen and eventually moved into the Mets starting rotation, going 6-17 for a Mets team that lost 111 games. In 1964, Stallard reduced his ERA by a full run per game but became a 20-game loser for that Mets team. He generally pitched better than his won-lost record, posting 11 complete games and 2 shutouts for his 10-20 record (3.79 ERA). Stallard also led the Mets staff with 118 strikeouts.

Stallard's persistence was rewarded when the Mets traded him and Elio Chacon to the St. Louis Cardinals for Johnny Lewis and Gordie Richardson. Pitching for the Cardinals in 1965, Stallard put together an 11-8 campaign with a 3.28 ERA. He was a versatile member of the Cardinals' staff, making 26 starts and 14 relief appearances. But his success in 1965 turned to disaster in 1966, as Stallard started the year 1-5 with a 5.68 ERA. He was reassigned to the Cardinals' Triple-A club at Tulsa, and pitched off and on in the minors through 1973, never earning a trip back to the big leagues.

Lee Stange

Lee Stange pitched in the major leagues for 10 years. He was signed in 1957 by the Washington Senators and made his major league debut in 1961 with the Minnesota Twins. Stange was 4-3 as a rookie in 1962, and went 12-5 for the Twins in 1963, posting a 2.62 ERA.

In 1964, he was traded to the Cleveland Indians for Jim "Mudcat" Grant, and was 8-4 for Cleveland in 1965 with a 3.34 ERA. In 1966, he

was traded with Don McMahon to the Boston Red Sox for Dick Radatz. He was 28-35 with a 3.45 ERA in 5 seasons with the Red Sox.

Stange was traded again in 1970, going to the Chicago White Sox, his last career stop. Stange finished with a 62-61 record and a 3.52 ERA.

Dick Stigman

Left-hander Dick Stigman won only 46 games in 7 major league seasons, but it wasn't for any particular lack of ability or drive on his part. Stigman was a tough competitor and a hard thrower whose won-lost record belied his effectiveness on the mound. Injuries and a lack of timely run support were the biggest challenges he faced in his all-too-short career.

A Minnesota native, Stigman was signed by the Cleveland Indians in 1954. He made his major league debut with the Tribe in 1960, and

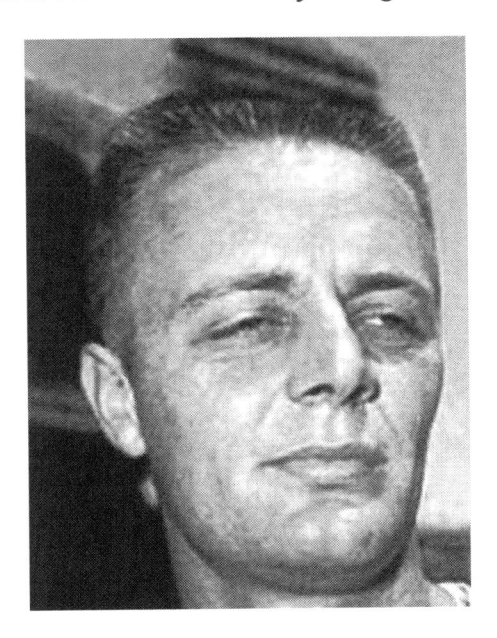

was selected to be part of the American League All-Star team as a rookie. He finished his first season at 5-11 with a 4.51 ERA as a starter and reliever. He started 18 games and finished 16 in relief, with 9 saves.

Injuries limited him to 22 appearances and a 2-5 record in 1961. The Indians traded Stigman (with Vic Power) to the Minnesota Twins for Pedro Ramos. Stigman went 12-5 in his first season with the Twins, posting a 3.66 ERA and leading all American League pitchers with a .706 winning percentage. In 1963, he went 15-15 with a 3.25 ERA and a career-high 241 innings pitched. His numbers for the 1963 season don't tell the whole story about his pitching that season. Seven of his 15 losses were one-run decisions. The Twins were shut out 4 times when Stigman started, and the team scored less than 3 runs for Stigman in 7 other starts. With a little more support (from a team known for its offensive firepower), Stigman easily could have won 20 games in 1963.

In 1964, his record slipped to 6-15 with a 4.03 ERA. But again, the Twins' bats seem to go silent when Stigman pitched. They were shut out during 5 of his starts, and scored less than 3 runs in 11 Stigman starts.

Injuries limited Stigman to a 4-2 record in 1965, and in the following off-season he was traded to the Boston Red Sox for Russ Nixon and Chuck Schilling. He was 2-1 for Boston as a starter-reliever in 1966, and then was dealt with Rollie Sheldon to the Cincinnati Reds. He would never pitch for Cincinnati, or for any other major league team. Stigman finished with a 46-54 record and a 4.03 ERA.

Tom Sturdivant

Right-hander Tom Sturdivant pitched for 7 different teams in 10 major league seasons. He was signed by the New York Yankees in 1948 and made his major league debut in 1955.

Sturdivant had back-to-back 16-win seasons for the Yankees starting in 1956, and his 16-6 record in 1957 led the major leagues with a .727 winning percentage. Working out of the bullpen, he was 9-5 for the Pittsburgh Pirates in 1962. Sturdivant retired after the 1964 season with a career record of 59-51 and a 3.74 earned run average.

Earl Wilson

Earl Wilson was a solid starting pitcher for the Boston Red Sox and Detroit Tigers during the 1960s. He also played a prominent role in baseball's transition to full integration during the 1950s.

A 6-foot-3, 215-pound right-hander who relied on sliders and fastballs, Wilson was signed by the Boston Red Sox in 1953, and debuted with the Red Sox in 1959. The Red Sox were the last American League team to break the color barrier when infielder Pumpsie Green made the club in 1959. Wilson made his major league debut with the Red Sox on July 31, 1959, as their first black pitcher. He joined the team's starting rotation in 1962  and averaged 11 victories per season from 1962 through 1965. Wilson threw a no-hitter against the Los Angeles Angels in 1962, the first African-American League pitcher to do so.

Midway through the 1966 season, Wilson was traded (with outfielder Joe Christopher) to the Detroit Tigers for outfielder Don Demeter and pitcher Julio Navarro. Wilson enjoyed his best seasons with the Tigers, winning 13 games over the rest of the 1966 season to finish 18-11 with a 3.07 ERA (2.59 with Detroit). He followed in 1967 with a 22-11 campaign, tying him for the league lead in victories with Cy Young Award winner Jim Lonborg.

Wilson started his baseball career as a catcher before switching to the pitching mound. He was one of the best hitting pitchers in baseball, swatting 35 career home runs (33 as a pitcher, fifth all time among major league pitchers).

Wilson won 25 games for the Tigers over the next 2 seasons, and closed out his career after splitting the 1970 season with Detroit and the San Diego Padres. He finished his career at 121-109 with a 3.69 ERA.

Earl Wilson
The first African-American to pitch a
no-hitter in the American League.

Wilbur Wood

Hall of Fame reliever Hoyt Wilhelm was not only the master of the knuckleball, but also its greatest evangelist. His promoting the pitch to bullpen teammates inspired at least 2 successful careers: one was the career of reliever Eddie Fisher, the other was the career of reliever-turned-starter Wilbur Wood.

Wood's career was going nowhere when Wilhelm advised him to rely on his knuckleball and not simply treat it as an occasional trick pitch. Wood had been signed by the Boston Red Sox in 1960 and pitched in the Bosox's minor league system for 5 years with only occasional stops in Beantown. He was purchased by the Pittsburgh Pirates in September of 1964 and finally won his first major league decision in 1965. He spent the 1966 season at the Pirates Triple-A affiliate in Columbus, going 15-8 before being traded to the Chicago White Sox for Juan Pizarro.

It was a trade that would change Wood's career. He met Wilhelm, and he listened. He went 4-2 for the White Sox in 1967 with a 2.42 ERA. That was 4-times as many major league games as he had previously won in his career.

In 1968 he set a major league record by appearing in 88 games, going 13-12 with a 1.87 ERA and 16 saves. In 1969 he made 76 appearances – all in relief – and went 10-11 with 15 saves. In 1970, his 77 relief appearances and 2.81 ERA produced a 9-13 record with 21 saves.

Then Wood made the last major transition of his career. He moved to the starting rotation, where the low physical stress of throwing the knuckleball allowed Wood to pitch more innings than any other starter in baseball – in fact more innings than any major league starter since the "Dead Ball" era prior to 1920. Wood went 22-13 in 1971 with a 1.91 ERA over 334 innings pitched. He averaged 21-16 with 45 starts and 348 innings per season from 1971 to 1975. And his earned run average over that period was 3.08.

Injury finally slowed Wood down, but it wasn't his arm that gave out. In May of 1976, Tigers center fielder Ron LeFlore hit a vicious line drive back at Wood, shattering his knee cap. He made a valiant effort to come back from the injury, but was never the same pitcher, going 17-18 over his final 2 seasons and retiring after the 1978 campaign.

Wood finished with a career record of 164-156 and a 3.24 ERA. He was an All-Star selection 3 times.

Al Worthington

Right-hander Al Worthington was a reliable reliever with 5 different teams over a 14-year major league career. He posted a career record of 75-82 with a 3.39 ERA and 110 saves. He was 11-7 for the San Francisco Giants in 1958, but his best all-around season came in 1965, when he was the bullpen ace of the American League champion Minnesota Twins.

Worthington was 10-7 with a 2.13 ERA and 21 saves in 1965. He led the American League with 18 saves in 1968 when he posted a 2.21

earned run average. In his final 6 seasons, all with the Twins, Worthington put up a combined record of 37-31 with 88 saves and an earned run average of 2.62.

John Wyatt

John Wyatt's major league career spanned the 1960s. He came up with the Kansas City Athletics in 1961, and retired after a brief tour with the Oakland A's in 1969. In between, he was one of the American League's busiest relief pitchers, and for most of the 1960s, one of the most effective.

He was signed by the St. Louis Cardinals in 1954 after pitching as a teenager in the Negro League. Wyatt bounced around the minors for 7 years (including a couple more Negro League stops). Kansas City purchased Wyatt in 1956 and brought him up for 5 games in 1961.

In 1962, as a 27-year-old rookie, Wyatt immediately established himself as the closer for the A's, appearing in 59 games and completing 30 of them with 11 saves. He was 10-7 for the ninth-place Athletics.

In 1963, Wyatt pitched in 63 games, all in relief, finishing 53 of them. He was 6-4 with 21 saves and a 3.13 ERA. In 1964, he set what was then a major league record with 81 pitching appearances, the first pitcher in the modern era to appear in at least half of his team's games. Wyatt was 9-8 that season with 20 saves and a 3.59 ERA. He was also a member of the American League All-Star team in 1964.

Wyatt pitched one more full season in Kansas City, going 2-6 in 1965 with 18 saves and a 3.25 ERA. In 1966, he was traded with Rollie Sheldon and Jose Tartabull to the Boston Red Sox for Jim Gosger,

Guido Grilli and Ken Sanders. He had an outstanding season with Boston in 1967, playing a major role in the team's pennant-winning performance. Wyatt was 10-7 with a 2.60 ERA, finishing 43 games in 60 appearances. (It was Wyatt's sixth straight season appearing in 60 or more games.) He had 20 saves during the regular season, and was the winning pitcher in Game 6 of the 1967 World Series.

Wyatt split the 1968 season between the Red Sox, the New York Yankees and the Detroit Tigers. He pitched in only 4 games for Oakland in 1969 before being released and retiring.

Wyatt helped solidify the role of the closing specialist, appearing in 389 games from 1962 through 1967, finishing 269 of them and recording 100 saves during those 6 seasons. He ended his 9-season career at 42-44 with a 3.47 ERA.

About the Author

Carroll Conklin combines a life-long passion for baseball with a three-decade career as a professional writer.

A graduate of Ashland University and Bowling Green State University, Carroll has spent more than 20 years as an advertising copywriter and marketing strategist. He has taught copywriting and brand theory at The Ohio State University and the Columbus College of Art & Design.

A prolific author, Carroll has also written books on topics ranging from marketing management to fear elimination.

He preaches the "gospel" of the 1960s as baseball's real golden age at www.1960sBaseball.com.

49469110R00069

Made in the USA
Lexington, KY
07 February 2016